CW00458093

Foreword

I first met Safaraz Ali whilst supporting charity and business mentoring initiatives alongside the very rewarding opportunity of judging the Asian Apprenticeship Awards which he founded. Our friendship since has been cemented and enriched by our shared passion to widen access to knowledge, experience and opportunity. Therefore, it is my pleasure to provide the foreword to the second instalment of the Canny Bites series: 'Another 52 Bites of Business Wisdom for Leaders and Entrepreneurs.'

I wholeheartedly recommend 'Another 52 Bites...' as a book that can help you recongise – and most importantly close – the gap between knowing 'it' and doing 'it'. In Safaraz's book, readers are guided from learning to actualising in the form of highly tangible and current bite sized examples. These purposeful 'bites' allow for a read that, although short in nature, is easy to understand and internalise, making the application of wisdom contained in the books that much more practical.

A must read for anyone looking to 'rock the boat' of common perceptions surrounding the nature of business and leadership; Safaraz's 'bites' provide an unmissable opportunity to broaden entrepreneurial horizons - from advice on how to thrive in the modern business world, to astute reflection on the 'self-made myth'. This is a book that sets out to stir direct action and challenge assumptions on every page. It forms a deeply introspective dive into the business world around us and how change is possible to reach the greatest success.

So, whether you are new to the art of business, looking to reflect on your current practice, or even looking for guidance on your future direction, 'Another 52 Bites of Business Wisdom...' will enable the learning that you can easily apply and adapt to your own personal circumstances. Easy to navigate, relevant, accessible, and fun – Safaraz will guide you throughout 'Another 52 Bites of Business Wisdom for Leaders and Entrepreneurs' to help you move from inspiration to actualisation.

Happy reading and, most importantly, happy actioning!

Sally Eaves

Prof. Sally Eaves.

Emergent Technology Expert, Futurist and Founder of Aspirational Futures

International Keynote Speaker and Award Winning Author

United Nations / Decade of Women Award Inaugural Winner for outstanding contribution to Frontier Technologies and Social Impact

www.sallyeaves.com
@sallyeaves

Testimonials

Safaraz has thought long and hard about establishing these 'Canny Bites' so that they can be used by anyone, from start-up business owners to established entrepreneurs of all ages. In a world of lifelong learning and constant change 'Another 52 Bites...' should be a welcome addition to anyone's library- especially those who wish to adapt and grow their own entrepreneurial and business practice.

- Rami Ranger CBE

Founder of Sun Mark Ltd

Founder of Sea, Air & Land Forwarding Ltd

Receiver of the Queens Award for Export Achievement 1999 and the Queen's Award for Enterprise 2009, 2010, 2011, 2012, 2013.

-

Essential reading for all business owners and leaders. Based off my own experience, many business books are often read once, then live out the rest of their lives forgotten about on a bookshelf. The second instalment of the 'Canny Bites' series understands this, and maintains its one-of-a-kind format to allow its readers to take manageable 'bites' of business wisdom in order to learn, and most importantly *apply* change to their own practice.

I highly recommend 'Another 52 Bites of Business Wisdom for Business Leaders and Entrepreneurs' as a book which drives you forward to take the movement both you and your business need.

- Paul Cadman

Finalist in EY's Entrepreneur of the Year 2016

Acquisition Internationals Most Innovative UK Leader 2016

Ambassador for the Education Awards

Birmingham Business Awards 'Man of the Year' 2017

Regardless of the size of your business, or what stage of the journey you are at, 'Another 52 Bites of Wisdom...' is inspired reading for all.
We live in a world of survival of the smartest and this book covers methods and strategies for today's entrepreneurs looking to make their mark in an increasingly competitive environment.

- Charlie Mullins OBE

Founder of Plimco Plumbers

Author of 'Bog-Standard Business - How I Took the Plunge and Became the Millionaire Plumber'

-

'Another 52 Bites of Wisdom for Business Leaders and Entrepreneurs' is one of the most accessible, informative, and insightful books for business leaders and entrepreneurs.

Its absolute best selling point is the simplification of various topics through a uniquely 'bite-sized' style of writing which gives its audience a keen desire to go out and research further, or to take direct planned and sustainable action in their professional lives. Most of all, 'Another 52 Bites...' inspires the inclination to succeed.

- Ninder Johal

Board Member West Midlands Growth Company

Board Governor University of Wolverhampton

Sandwell College Vice Chairman of the Board

Preface

Once again, I find myself sitting down to write a preface to a book. With my second title now complete and on its way to the publishers, and my mind already moving onto what's next, I've been thinking a lot recently about the concept of 'busyness' and what it means to be truly busy. In business, it's easy to often find ourselves preoccupied with a million different things (in fact, the word 'business' started life in the Middle Ages to describe the state of being busy, and was used as such until the 18th century!), but adding another string to your bow means nothing if you're not able to hit the target.

The majority of people will happily talk about being busy. They'll harp on about simply getting stuff done. They may attend seminars on decision-making, go to networking events to meet people, and do extensive research and reading on a certain topic. But these people will happily read a book to learn something new, even going as far as to make plenty of notes, and then... nothing happens.

These people do not take direct action. They will not change anything. Instead, they make excuses, and can often be heard saying that they need to wait for 'X' to happen before they can do 'Y'.

Then there are the others. From my personal perspective, I have noticed a common trait in the most successful entrepreneurs and leaders, and often this trait is what makes them who they are. It's their relentless focus on doing something, taking action, and getting "stuff" done.

It's not enough for them to be passive and take on board knowledge and information without leveraging it. To them, knowledge only really matters when it makes a difference and when they can do something as a result. It could be changing the way they implement a process or complete a task. It may be a change in their tactics or strategy. It may be the spark that makes them finally sit down and start writing their own book. These people – who learn and then act, only to move onto learning again – are the true entrepreneurs.

And that's what my second 'Canny Bites' book is about. I've created this book with the aim of inspiring action. In a slight departure from my last book - which focused on learning from narrative - this book focuses on key takeaways which can help you to take action. From tips to sell your product or services, help designing a strong USP, questions to help you find your purpose, and notes on how to work with a business consultant - each bite is designed to help you do something. Whatever it is. And if you do, then my job is done.

Safaraz Ali

Canny Bites

Another 52 bites of business wisdom
for leaders and entrepreneurs

Safaraz Ali

Contents

Everything starts with you

As with most things in the world of entrepreneurship, growing your business starts with **you**. How can you expect your team to grow your business, or your clients to put their trust in your services, if you don't have the correct mindset to start with? In this chapter, we will discuss what makes a leader and help you answer the question *are you cut out to run a business?*

1. Are you cut out to run a business?
2. Leadership: nature or nurture?
3. The difference between a manager and a leader
4. Some thoughts on leadership

1. Are you cut out to run a business?

Written in 1995, 'The E-Myth Revisited' by Michael E. Gerber explores the reason why most small businesses simply don't work.

Gerber argues that in order for a small business to be a success, the owner needs to understand the 3 key roles that they must play - the technician, the manager, and the entrepreneur. The entrepreneur dreams visions, sets goals, and implements strategies, the manager looks for ways to build processes and operations to set the wheels in motion and keep them turning, and the technician is focused on technical implementation. The essence of the E-Myth – or the entrepreneurial myth – is that most small businesses are started by technicians, rather than entrepreneurs. In other words, they're started by people who are very good at what they do, but who lack the business know-how and inclination to sell their products and grow their business.

But is the E-myth still relevant today? Much has changed in the last 25 years – the technology that we use today, for example, didn't exist when Gerber penned his influential book. These days, readily available content and information means people can educate themselves on any topic they desire. Forums and social media allow individuals to grow their networks easily and instantly, and online tools for things such as marketing or accounts help entrepreneurs to manage their business with ease. It's easy to see why, in many respects, much of what Gerber's book talks about is perhaps not as relevant today.

However, no matter how much changes around us, one thing has always remained the same: the human mind.

Perhaps the key takeaway from the E-Myth isn't about your business model and how to run it, but how new business owners must develop the mindset of an entrepreneur. Technical know-how is crucial, but it isn't enough to make your business a success.

It can be hard to shift from approaching problems in the same way you have always done, but as an entrepreneur it's crucial that you develop the skills to look beyond the problem that's in front of you. The good thing is that today's technology makes it easier than ever - you just need the drive to take on the challenge.

2. Leadership: nature or nurture?

This is a question that is often debated, and in reality there are often elements of both. Some people are natural leaders. Others aren't and have no desire to be. Then there are those in between, who have few natural leadership skills, but want to learn to become a leader.

Business owners tend to fall into the first and last categories, but regardless of where you find yourself on this spectrum, it's important to always be honing your skills. As John F. Kennedy once said, "Leadership and learning are indispensable to each other."

Here are a few ways you can nurture the leader in you:

Ask yourself, 'Am I ready to lead?'
Successful leaders are driven and motivated. If you're not quite confident enough to lead, you'll lack this drive and motivation, which can impact on your growth and success. So how do you figure out if you're ready? A good test is to acknowledge any hesitancies you may have about leading. Write down your doubts and worries about leadership, and work through how, or if, you can overcome them.

Know what qualities a good leader in your sector should possess
There's a general consensus of what a leader should be; decisive, confident, and inspirational, to name a few ideas. But which leaderships skills are important in your industry? For example,

in a very fast-paced setting, decisiveness may be highly valued, whereas a slower-paced creative environment may hold an inspirational leader in higher esteem. Identifying these and building them into your leadership style is key to establishing yourself and your business within your sector.

Never stop learning to lead

Even if you're a natural born leader and have been leading teams and businesses for years, your learning should always be ongoing. It can be easy to lose motivation if you've been in the same leadership role for a long time, or if you take on a new venture in which you need to adapt your skills, but leadership is one of the hottest topics in business, which means there's a wealth of learning material available to get you inspired. Seek them out and keep developing your leadership skills.

3. The difference between a manager and a leader

We've already looked at the different skills and personas a business owner needs to master, but quite often, those who aspire to be a great leader fall short and end up simply being a great manager. The fact is, not all managers are necessarily leaders. The art of managing people is indeed an important skill, but the ability to lead people is something that not all managers achieve – even if they are good at what they do. As such, although the roles are interdependent, it's important to understand the differences between the two.

Managers are good at making decisions - They gather the right information, come to a solid conclusion, and delegate actions effectively.

Leaders create good decision makers - They ask the right questions and encourage their team and others to reach the right conclusions independently.

Managers develop performance - They do this by identifying what others are *good at* and helping them to reach their targets.

Leaders develop talent - They do this by identifying what others *enjoy doing* and helping them to work towards achieving their full potential.

Managers keep the wheels turning - They ensure that tasks are done on time and to a good standard. They make mistakes, but learn from them and are consistent in their approach to new challenges.

Leaders drive change - Leaders don't just embrace challenges - they seek them. They're not afraid of trying new things and they're not afraid of failing - they simply see it as a learning opportunity and an essential element of growth. They encourage those around them to face challenges in this way, too.

How can you move forward to become a better leader?

4. Some thoughts on leadership

When people try to define a leader, they often think of the charismatic person standing at the front of the room, saying something worthy and inspiring. But are all leaders like that?

The answer is of course not. So why, when we imagine leaders, is this what we think of? In reality, there are many different kinds of leaders. There are so many, in fact, that we give the different types certain names . Not all of them I would particularly agree with, but a few examples include: autocratic leaders, directors, servant leaders, hard leaders, passive leaders, dynamic leaders, collaborative leaders, uninspiring leaders, those who lead-from-the-front or lead-from-behind – to name just a few.

The stereotypical image of a leader is simply a photoshopped image – it's good for the videos and TV shows, but not so good when put into practice. True leadership is about pursuing the vision, not bragging about it. True leaders are more likely to be found in a back room, helping to plan out new products or campaigns, talking to staff and to customers, as opposed to fronting the show all the time.

In my experience, some of the most inspiring and compelling leaders I've worked with have been the shy and retiring types. They are the ones most likely to naturally shun from the limelight. They simply know what they need to do, and they get on with it. They don't seek the glory but understand at times they will need to stand at the front.

But why does this matter?

Leadership is not about mission statements. It's about leading people. And those people depend on their leaders to guide them to success so that they can do rewarding jobs in a well-managed team. They rely on them to create a safe environment where they can do their best, try out new ideas and learn from their mistakes without blame or reprimand. They are not looking for someone to lead them to glory, but someone to lead them in creating their own achievements.

Three skills to help you thrive in the modern business world

The business world is constantly changing. In this increasingly connected world, business owners and leaders need to get to grips with the latest trends and technologies now more than ever. Here are some important skills every business leader should master in the coming years.

5. Content creation: content is king
6. Live broadcasting: raw and authentic you
7. Data: your most powerful currency

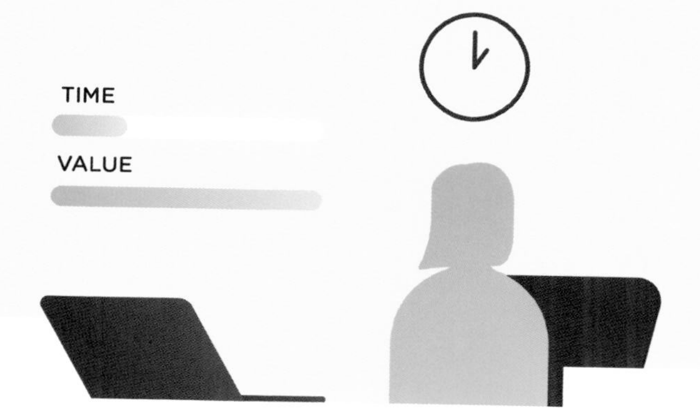

5. Content creation: content is king

According to the Content Marketing Institute, content marketing is:

'the strategic marketing approach of creating and distributing valuable, relevant and consistent content to attract and acquire a clearly defined audience – with the objective of driving profitable customer action'

Every business is sitting on expertise that can be translated into valuable content. The key is figuring out what you have, what you can create, and what you can repurpose. This is an important part of content creation – the ability to recreate and repurpose content. It may have started as an email to someone explaining the benefits of a new tool, but with a bit of work it can become a PowerPoint, a blog, or a video.

There are many different forms of content marketing, but I would suggest that it's crucial for every business leader to get to grips with these in order to get the most out of their expertise.

Blogging - although our attention span for reading continues to dwindle, a well-written blog post is still a great medium for giving value to your audience. It's also a way to keep your website current and to bring traffic to your site. You can also share your views and thoughts as part of building confidence in you and your business by blogging on 3rd party platforms such as LinkedIn or Medium. Also, don't think once your blog is published, it's magically going to get exposure. Distribution of your blog is as important as writing it in the first place - share on social media, email it to people, and repurpose it where possible.

Video and audio - Jay Baer, entrepreneur and content marketing expert, recently declared 'video is the new blogging', and for many businesses, this is true. Different formats will appeal to different audiences - video and audio being particularly stimulating over longer pieces of text. So, once you've mastered blogging, why not consider repurposing your content into a video or podcast?

Infographics - All businesses can deal in data these days – a simple survey of your customers can give you the necessary information to create an exciting infographic. You don't even need to get a designer in these days – there are plenty of free tools online to help you create graphics.

6. Live broadcasting: raw and authentic you

This millenia, video is big. Do you know what's even bigger?

Live video.

Recent years have seen many live broadcasting services pop up, with social media giants hopping on the live bandwagon. Despite this, many business owners are still steering clear of it, and not harnessing the power of live broadcasting.

It's understandable – live broadcasting is nerve-wracking. You're putting yourself, and your business, out there. But anything can be nerve-wracking to start with, and there are many benefits to be reaped from hitting that 'live' button – stats show that people will spend **3x longer watching a video if it's live.** Here are a few tips to make sure that you're ready for your close up.

Prepare, practice, and test - Prepare your broadcast, just as you would with any content creation. If possible, create a script and whittle it down to prompt words. Remember, prepare for any questions that could come your way, and be sure to answer them – if not, you may just as well have pre-recorded a video instead!

Ask for feedback - Before your first broadcast, try recording yourself and watching back to see how you come across. Ask trusted colleagues, peers, or even a small sample of your target audience for their honest feedback – did they find the video of any value and is it engaging, for example? Their feedback will be a strong indicator of how your audience will perceive you.

Make it personal and engage - It's important to attach that personal touch to a live broadcast. Make some time to say a bit about yourself at the beginning of the video, and if possible greet new people who log in to watch. This makes viewers feel more welcome and part of the session, and also gives them a call to action to engage and watch again once the broadcast is over.

Don't expect perfection - Someone may throw you a curveball question that you weren't expecting, so don't pretend you know how to answer it perfectly. There's no shame in saying you're not sure right now but you'd be happy to pick it up with them at a later date. Remember, this is live broadcasting, so there are plenty of things that could go wrong, such as technical issues – just take everything in your stride and don't panic if something happens.

Chew on this:

What could you share with your audience in a live broadcast right now?

7. Data: your most powerful currency

Data is transforming the nature of business in fundamental ways – it's become a bit of buzzword these days, and for a good reason. Data can help you gain a competitive advantage, all you need to do is harness the power of your customers' curiosity.

Here's how harnessing the power of data can help your business:

Understand customer needs better - The ability to analyse big data enables you to truly know your customers. What are their likes and dislikes? How much money do they generally spend? What time of year do they make the most purchases? Utilising big data gives you a full customer profile, allowing you to interact with the customer in a way you are confident they will respond to.

Personalise your campaigns - Sometimes marketing can feel like a bit of a guessing game. You may think your customers will like a certain campaign, but do you have any evidence to support that? Having the right data and using it allows you to create personal and relevant campaigns that will speak loud and clear to the customer.

Predict the next trends - Looking at your customers' purchase patterns will help your business to predict what they want next. This is not only good news for your business from a product or service development perspective, but is great news for the customer who gets something they want before they've even realised they want it!

Using data internally - Peter Drucker, management guru, said: ‘you can’t manage what you can’t measure’. Drucker is spot-on – how can you know if your business is successful unless success is defined and tracked by data?

Whether your weapon of choice is big data, small data, structured data, or something else entirely, your business’s data is your currency – use it!

Chew on this:

What data do you have at your fingertips right now and are you aware of your GDPR obligations? How could you use this to your benefit?

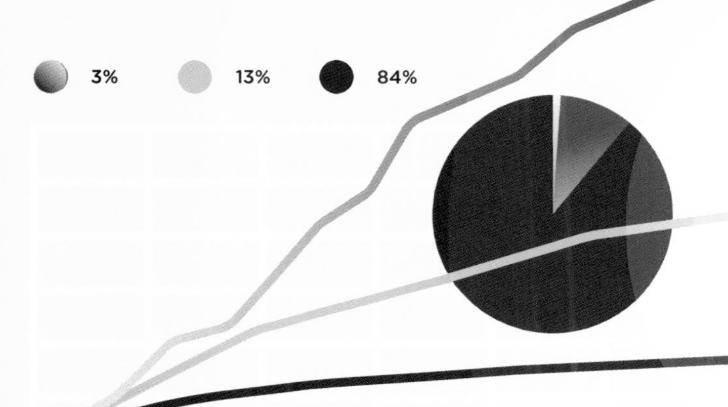

Communicate up to stand out

Who are you? What is your business? How do you spread the word and get people to truly believe in what you're offering them? This chapter is all about your message – defining what it is, how you put value on it, and how you can share it.

8. What is your backstory?

9. People first, business second

10. Is it time to ditch your USP?

11. Testing your USP

12. Digitalisation: how content helps you clone

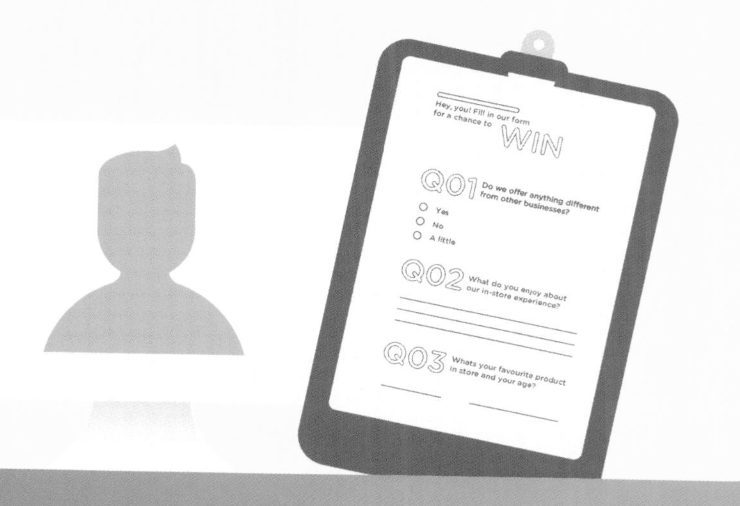

8. What is your backstory?

We often assume that our customers and partners are focused on 'Me, Myself, and I'. This means that we often take a WIIFT – or 'What's In It For Them?.' approach to our business communications.

Yes, in today's world, you must be in the business your customers want you to be in. If you don't carry a product that gives them the benefit or solution they seek – if you don't provide a service that thoroughly encompasses just what they're looking for – they are going to take their business elsewhere. But has anyone ever asked you 'what's your story'?

For any business, the key to good working relationships with clients is a mutual understanding of the 'why?' on both parts. So while we, as business leaders, are often focused on understanding our client's 'why', we must place an equal importance on getting them to understand our 'why'.

How can we do this? All business owners need to ensure that their team don't just know what the business does, but why it does it.

Your 'why' is a powerful tool, and properly communicating it to your employees can be very empowering. A good 'why' should drive your team to feel motivated and enthusiastic about each day at work. They should feel excited to share your business's story and to do good work. By doing this, your employees will be able to effectively communicate your 'why' to your customers. Once they understand your motivations, your customers won't just buy **what** you do, but **why** you do it and trust in you even more.

Your backstory is powerful. Share it.

Chew on this:
What's your backstory? How can you communicate this better with your customers?

NOW

9. People first, business second

'Community' is an overused word, but it's often overlooked in business. Most people belong to a community of some kind – whether it relates to a hobby, celebrates an artist or entertainer that they are a fan of, or simply connects local people together. Communities create a space for engagement, education, and reach – so it's important that businesses leverage their power.

Here are a few ways to create and utilise a community around your business:

- **Understand the benefits** – Communities create increased loyalty as they establish a more personal relationship between customer and business.
- **The power of social** – Social media groups are an easy and powerful way of bringing people together. Look for opportunities to create communities around your customers' interests and needs. LinkedIn and Facebook are great for this, but remember – it is not where the community is but what you actually do in that community that counts.
- **Be active – but not too active** – The best communities work when they are exactly that – communities. To get the best value from a community, you cannot be in charge of everything. Let the members of the community run it as if it is theirs, but remember to interact with them regularly, too.

- **Rethink face-to-face** – Online communities are great, but face-to-face communities, such as networking or mastermind groups, can encourage mutual support and build long-lasting connections – something that can't always be done solely online.

- **People first** – People will always respond more positively to genuine human interaction than anything else, so remember to put community first and commerce second.

Chew on this:

How can you build and grow a community around your business?

10. Is it time to ditch your USP?

The truth is, often your unique selling point isn't really all that unique.

We offer a truly great service!
We always put the customer first!
We're experts in our field!
We offer great value for money!

These claims are often made by many businesses as unique selling points, but cannot be unique as they are shared statements that almost all businesses will make at some point. Take a look at them again. How often have you heard these? Do any of these 'unique' selling points really sound unique to you?

While these promises are all good, they're also what every other business says. This means that they might be good at helping you attract new customers, but there's very little that is likely to make them stay. If your USP is the the same as everybody else's, what's stopping your customers moving to another business who can offer them the same service?

Having a clear proposition is better than trying to be 'all things to all people.'

For example, Ryanair has a very clear and distinct proposition that makes it one of the biggest aviation business success stories. It doesn't promise a great in-flight experience, excellent food, or seat-back TV screens. What it does offer is a very clear proposition – price. And this isn't an arbitrary marketing message in the way that all businesses claim to offer a good price – Ryanair is run based upon a 'low cost' ethos which rigorously ensures it can offer prices that can't be matched by any of the other major airlines.

Your USP doesn't have to be crazy to make you stand out – it just needs to be about what you **do** rather than what you **say**. A true USP should be measurable by objective standards, rather than something that is subjective. For example, what is great value for money to you may not be to someone else. Take a look at what you do best. Is it measurable? Objective? If not, ditch it and be better!

11. Testing your USP

As we've discovered, not all USPs truly are USPs - the word is often overused, especially when it comes to things that are quite difficult to truly be unique in, such as customer service. But it is possible to have a USP, and where you have identified one, it needs to be tested.

Anyone who has seen Dragon's Den knows that having a USP looks good – in fact, those businesses who are unable to provide a USP to the Dragons are often portrayed as doomed to fail. However, a USP is not about making your business appear attractive – it's about what it helps you to provide your customer. Here's how to tell if your USP is up to scratch.

Is your USP relevant to your customer?

It may be obvious, but that's the reason businesses overlook it. Your USP must address the needs and concerns of your customer. There's no point being the cheapest on the market if your audience is concerned with high quality service. Even less so if they're willing to pay for it! Your USP, therefore, must be relevant, and it must be fit for purpose. The key is to understand your audience. Get into their frame of mind. What things are important to them? Explore your customers' needs, test the effectiveness of your solutions, and tailor your USP to meet those needs. Perhaps hold a brainstorming session where you identify your typical customers' needs or run a survey and gather feedback from your audience. Review regularly to ensure that your USP is still important to your audience – changes in your business or industry might have an effect on your customers' priorities.

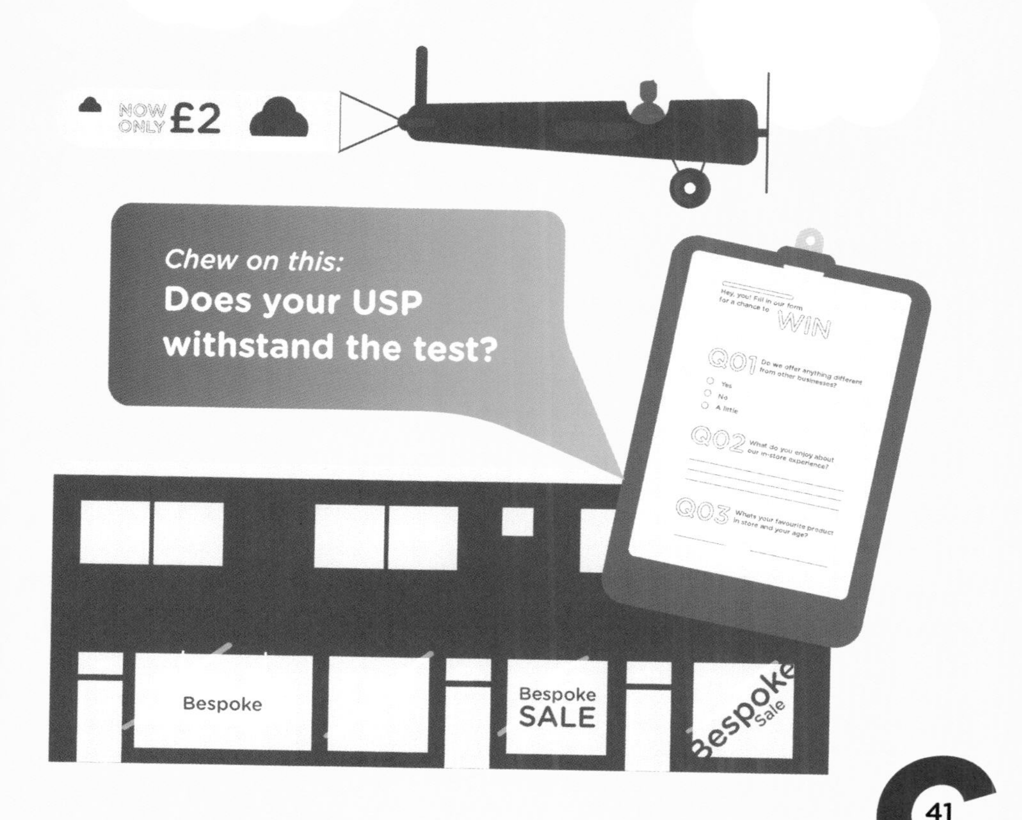

12. Digitalisation: how content helps you clone

Imagine, thousands of years ago, you discovered how to start a fire. To share your knowledge, you would have had to call people around you and physically demonstrate it live. This limited the number of people you could tell about your new knowledge, as you and your audience both had to physically be present. Knowledge tended to stay local, unless someone else took the time to travel and share a discovery.

These days, you no longer have to pitch to the gatekeepers. You can go straight to your audience. Or rather, they can come to you.

Everyone who is looking to sell something knows how important relationships are. The more people who know, like, and trust you, the more you are likely to sell. In essence, convincing people to buy is about educating them about the benefits of your product or services.

But you don't have to physically build a relationship with one person at a time to educate them about your expertise – content allows you to 'clone yourself' and address all your prospects and customers at once. You no longer have to be interviewed on television to reach a large audience, you just need to produce and digitalise ideas, thoughts, processes, and much more.

You must always look out for new things to learn and share with your audience and improve the quality of your ideas. Content lets you clone yourself in that you can reach as many people as possible, but it is also our biggest opportunity to stand out as an individual and differentiate ourselves from the rest of the marketplace.

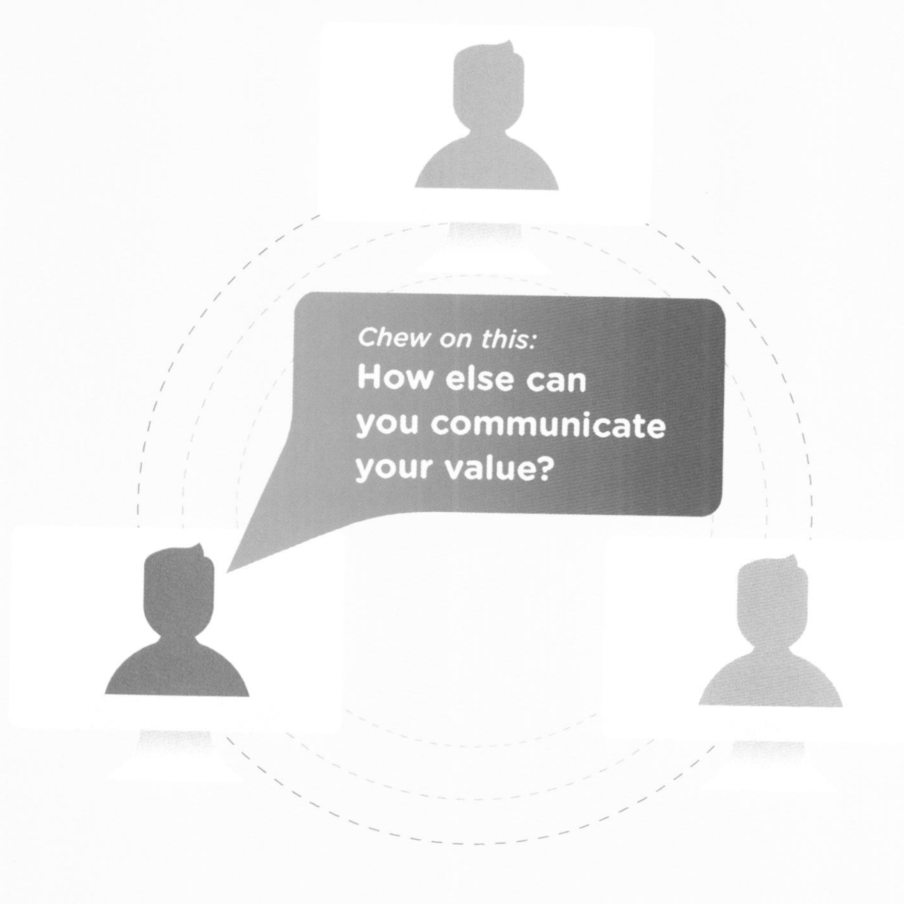

The Kipling six and other questions that need answers

Starting and running your own business inevitably comes with lots of questions. What kind of leader am I? What is my business' purpose? What do I need to help me grow my business? All of us have asked or will ask ourselves these questions in our journey, so in this chapter we take a look at how you can go about tackling them.

13. Let's begin with the Kipling six

14. Business consultants: charlatans or gurus?

15. Numbers, but which numbers?

16. Are you a hedgehog or a fox?

13. Let's begin with the Kipling six

"I keep six honest serving-men
They taught me all I knew;
Their names are What and Why and When
And How and Where and Who."

Rudyard Kipling's famous poem 'Six Honest Serving Men' is often quoted in business training programmes to help business leaders find their purpose and goals. Although they're not necessarily in the right order, the poem is a great way to help you know where you are and plan where you want to be.

Who am I now? – Ask yourself who you are at this point in time. What sort of person are you, and what do you mean to those around you?

Where have I been? – Look at your journey – your ups and downs. What has influenced your development over the years?

What do I want? – What is your vision? How has this changed over time?

Why do I want it? – What will reaching your goals help you to achieve?

When do I want it? - Bill Gates famously said, "Most people overestimate what they can do in one year and underestimate what they can do in ten years". Look carefully at your goal and your steps to get there. What needs to happen by when? What steps rely on the contribution and completion of others?

How am I going to make it happen? Ideas are easy - implementation is hard. Make sure you have the tools, knowledge, and support to help you achieve your goals. And if you don't - go and get them.

14. Business consultants: charlatans or gurus?

A consultant is someone who borrows your watch to tell you the time, and then keeps your watch... or so the old joke goes.

Many individuals may be sceptical about the value a business consultant brings to an organisation, but the simple truth is companies that are growing or facing difficulties need to tap into a wealth of knowledge and experience that they may simply not possess at that time.

Experienced and proven business management consultants draw on their expertise, working with numbers of other successful businesses to get to the point of what really matters. Using one means you can draw on their specific skills and sector experience to...

- Focus on the things that will help you grow
- Build rigorous systems
- Develop clear strategic business plans focused on actions
- Obtain invaluable knowledge for a new or growing business

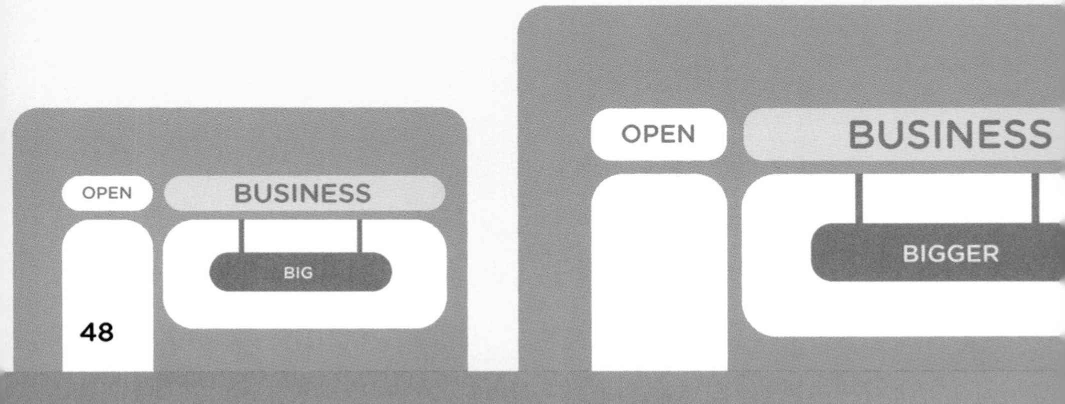

Statistics show that nearly **half of startups** fail within the first 3 years, and not many of those which do survive manage to hit their initial goals and aspirations. Those that do face certain growing pains.

Taking advantage of robust tools and techniques, combined with the expertise and experience that the consultant brings, can deliver measurable results and help businesses survive in a world of constant change.

Chew on this:
How could a business consultant help you grow?

15. Numbers, but which numbers?

Being a business owner brings many challenges and responsibilities – the overriding responsibility being always to act in the best interests of the company. This presents personal, as well as legal and financial risks. Therefore, you must be able to make informed decisions. But how do you do that?

Often, a business consultant is essential for a new, growing, or changing business, as they will help you set the foundations for the future. But how do you get the most out of your business consultant? **It's all in the numbers.**

You cannot control what you don't measure, so one of the first things that will happen is that the consultant will ask you about your numbers. Take some time to think about what things you are already measuring, what things you are not measuring, and

what things you probably should be measuring. Together, you will critically assess which numbers *truly* matter.

This is the most important step when working with a business consultant, as without understanding and measuring your numbers, you will never know what the true driving force of your business is. Once you have this down, you can build the dashboard, or barometer, for your business, evaluate performance of products and services, understand the critical timings in your business plan, seek to mitigate risks, and successfully and fully direct the affairs of the company.

Understanding your numbers is the first step and number one priority in working out which numbers really matter.

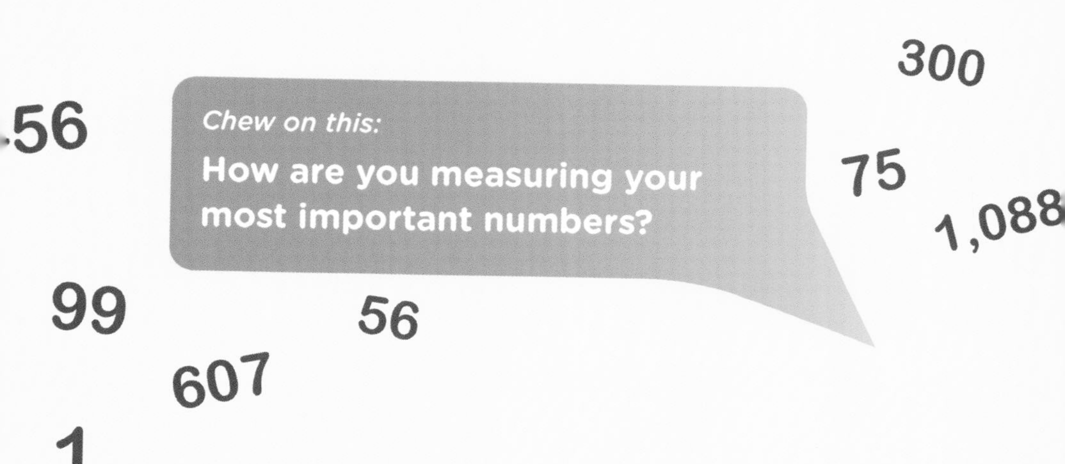

16. Are you a hedgehog or a fox?

If you could choose to be a fox or a hedgehog, which would you rather be? Most people would choose to be a fox, as they are quick and cunning, but what if I told you that you should be the hedgehog?

In 2001, Jim Collins published his influential book, 'Good to Great'. In the book, he developed the idea of the Hedgehog Concept, based on an ancient Greek parable that states: 'The fox knows many things, but the hedgehog knows one big thing.'

Foxes are clever animals, but they pursue many different goals at once. They have many different strategies, and work through them quickly in a way that can appear scattered and unfocused. This can have a negative effect on what they are trying to achieve in the long run.

Hedgehogs, on the other hand, are slow, steady, and unassuming. However, they are good at one thing, which helps them to achieve their goal of survival: they are very good at defending themselves.

Collins argues that 'hedgehogs' in the business world are good at achieving their goals by doing one thing, and doing it well. But how can you identify this one thing?

First, you must make 3 simple assessments:

- What is your business passionate about?
- What is your business best at?
- Where is your business generating the most revenue?

In order to find your 'Hedgehog Concept', you will need to identify the sweet spot in the middle of these three things, and focus on it. But it is important to understand that a key part of the 'Hedgehog Concept' is not a goal or strategy to be the best at this thing, but an understanding of **what** you can be the best at, and **how** you can get there.

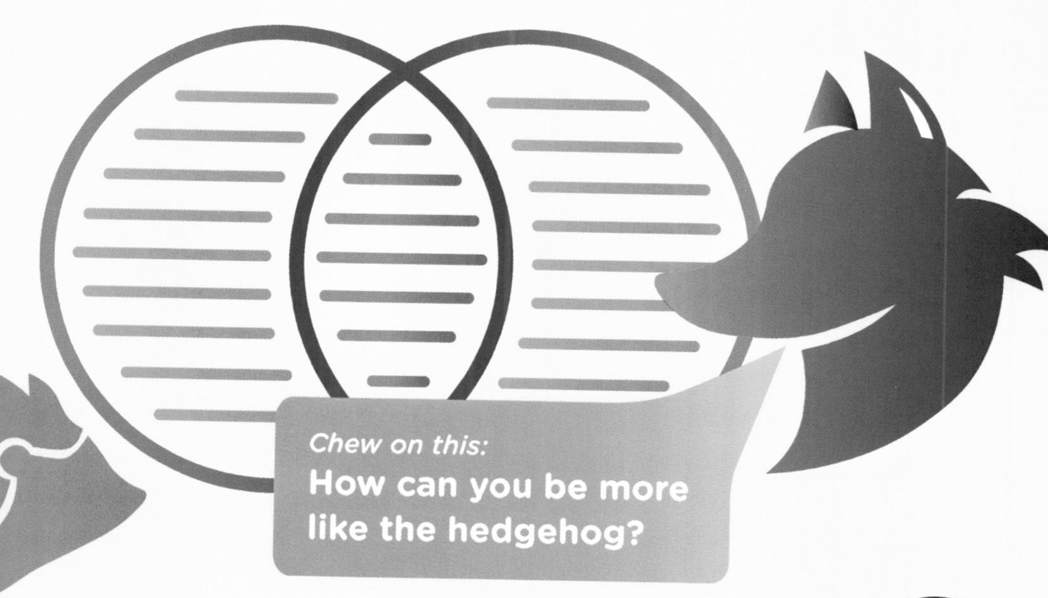

The self-made myth

No individual is an island, and no individual is a business. A successful business is made up of many different people - both inside and outside of your organisation - and therefore it's key to always have the right people by your side to support you as your business grows, and to help you develop new opportunities. There is no such thing as a self-made person - it's simply a myth! Without the help of others, what can you achieve on your own?

17. Your team, your reflection

18. Mentoring: it's a two way street

19. Leveraging the power of communities

20. Co-operative hunting for your business

17. Your team, your reflection

Here's a secret only the best leaders and business owners know.

Your team is not just a means for you to execute your master plan. They're not there to simply get the job done, to do the work for you, or to help you reach your revenue target.

Yes, your team is responsible for the day-to-day running of your business, but they actually serve a much more important function than that.

Your team is actually your feedback mechanism, your mirror. You may often think about your role as a business leader in giving feedback to your team, but how can you do that without first being able to reflect on what you have taught them, and if you have taught them well? For example, many leaders are convinced that they are great communicators, yet can't understand why they're being ignored by their team. The reality is that they simply aren't saying anything that their team are able to hear. It's almost as if they have been speaking a different language the whole time.

Accountability is important in business, and the biggest lesson that a business leader must learn is that when their staff do not perform in a way that is expected of them, they are accountable. Your team is a reflection of you and your leadership. Looking at this reflection, analysing it, and changing what you don't like will ultimately make you a better leader.

Your team are an extension of you. Your eyes and your ears. Your senses that will inform your ability to navigate towards your vision.

18. Mentoring: it's a two-way street

It is the famous science fiction writer Robert Heinlein who is credited with coining the term, 'when one teaches, two learn', but unlike his other writing, there is nothing fictional or unbelievable about what is meant by this saying. In fact, there is an undeniable truth in it, which is why it is crucial to look for opportunities to share your knowledge in order to be successful. For business leaders, there is no better way to teach than by becoming a mentor and, in my opinion, no better way to learn. Whether or not you want to run a formal mentoring scheme, surrounding yourself with potential mentees is a crucial part of building a support system that will enable you to grow.

So how can you benefit from mentoring?

Consolidating your knowledge

You have to know a topic inside and out before you can properly teach it to another person. However, in passing on your learning, you are not just consolidating your technical or industry knowledge, but you are also building confidence in your own – and your mentee's - expertise.

Gaining perspective

You won't always know the answer to every question you get asked, and sometimes somebody will approach you with an issue that requires you to ask questions before you can give an answer.

Although you may feel like this means you aren't well equipped enough to answer the question, it is actually giving you some important information – context about your business.

Keeping up to date

During his time as General Electric CEO, Jack Welch set up a reverse mentoring programme which enabled his younger staff to teach older members about computer systems. This is a great reminder that working with people of different ages and backgrounds, who may have different experiences and knowledge, gives you a resource which you can draw on to develop your own skills and keep you up to date.

Learning to lead

Mentoring helps you gain critical leadership skills, such as how to bring out the best in others, recognise strengths and weaknesses, and how to help others achieve great results.

Chew on this:

Look around you - who in your network could you mutually learn from?

19. Leveraging the power of communities

Groups and communities can help us to identify who we are and what we stand for, but they also illustrate who we are *not*.

There are many everyday examples of this in action, which demonstrate the power of groups in varying extremes. For example, consider the ways in which the act of identifying with one football team as opposed to another can inspire both pride and hatred in a supporter; or how favouring one brand of washing powder over another can create perceived differences – even if they were made in the same factory.

Many groups and identities are arbitrary, but they are powerful enough to influence people's thoughts and feelings.

Identity and communities are a wonderful thing in the business world. But quite often, we run the risk of cordoning ourselves off from great opportunities when we decide we are one thing and not another. The key to growing your business and exposing yourself to more people is to be open minded and diverse.

Chew on this:
What groups do you know that could be of benefit to you?

Try joining as many clubs and societies as you can – time and resource permitting – even if they might not seem entirely relevant at first. Find out how you can influence the feelings of others within those groups. This is a great way to grow your business, become more influential, and appeal to people on opposite ends of a spectrum. If you find that a particular group doesn't offer you great benefits, that's fine – but keep in touch if possible. You never know what might come out of it.

20. Co-operative hunting for your business

As the saying goes, 'birds of a feather flock together'.

One of the most effective ways of winning, doing business and making new connections, is to form strategic partnerships with other businesses. Allying with those who may operate in your sector or market can actually work to a mutual benefit. Understanding and adopting this approach can be a key game changer for your business and can help it to grow at a faster pace.

We've talked before about the **'Wedding Mafia'**... this is when planners, dress shops, florists, car hire businesses, venues, photographers, and caterers team up to work together. When one of them gets wedding business, they bring in the others, making it difficult for anyone outside of the 'mafia' to get referrals.

One of the key mindset changes you must undergo as a business owner, is not to always see other businesses as threats, but as opportunities. Start by actively looking to network with other businesses and consultants who operate within your industry, but who perhaps have other specialisms or audiences to yours.

In forming strategic alliances, referring to one another, and supporting each other in the supply chain activity, you can go for bigger contracts and also offer additional services that you couldn't before. By doing this, you will gradually begin to find that more business now comes from your partners rather than directly from other sources.

In essence, strategic alliances and partnerships are one of the best weapons a small business can have in their arsenal, as they bring huge benefits at very little cost.

Chew on this:

What other business do you know that could be part of your strategic alliance?

Creating a culture for success

Success doesn't simply come from a gifted individual or working hard, although both are important. It is about creating something that is greater than the sum of its component parts. It's about creating an environment in which all can contribute and feel valued. A success culture is a set of values, actions, and behaviours that should be preserved and cultivated for growth.

21. A little competition never hurt anyone
22. The three Hs of hiring
23. Entrepreneurship within a business: embracing intrapreneurship
24. Influencing intrapreneurship in your business
25. Taking the con out of conflict
26. The benefits of diversity
27. Unlocking the potential of a diverse team
28. Matching employee experience to employer brand
29. Setting the foundation for business transformation
30. Netflix culture
31. Help! My high-performing team member has taken another job

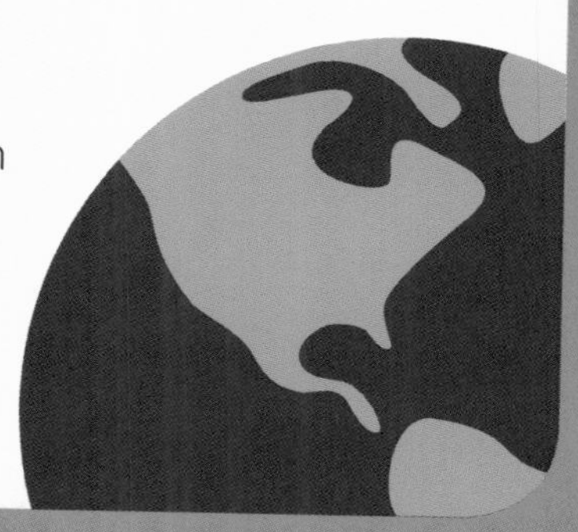

21. A little competition never hurt anyone

How many times have you said **'great job team'**, **'star player'** or **'man of the match'?**

We often talk about our colleagues and peers using sporting metaphors. We are, after all, a team, right?

But have you ever thought about the benefits of competition **within** your business or team? Teamwork and equality aims to create harmony, accord, and a great work culture. Competition, however, creates great individuals who achieve results. Competition can inspire people to get better and work harder.

A little competition in your business, managed in the right way, might be a great way to inspire a culture that values self-improvement and a desire to hit targets. Doing so in a creative and fun way can help to stimulate an environment where everybody wants to contribute to your business's goals.

Business, as they say, is the sport people play when they get older. The key, however, is to remember that you're all still on the same team at the end of the day.

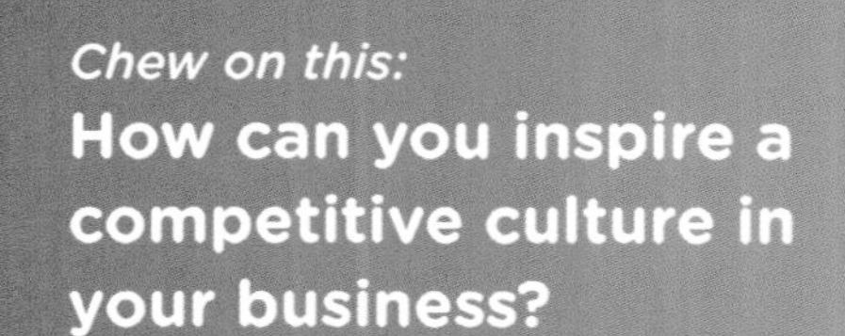

I thought we were on the same side! Why are we competing?

Yes, we are. It's for the betterment of the team!

REAT JOB TEAM • ST

22. The three H's of hiring

When hiring somebody new to join your business, what do you look for?

For many people, the right skills and knowledge are the most essential thing when considering a candidate's application for a position. But how often do you think about behaviours, values, and whether the person will be suited to your business and its culture?

The three H's of hiring is a way of ensuring that when somebody signs on the dotted line of their new contract of employment, you can be sure that they will fit right in with your other employees and correspond with the standards that you set for the business.

These are:

Habits

Throwing a cannonball into your office is likely to disrupt your other employees. Consider whether the person has good habits. Would they be able to follow systems and processes? Are they organised and likely to work in harmony with your existing team, meaning they can work together seamlessly?

Hunger

Tony Robbins, author and entrepreneur, once said, "passion is first gear; it will get you going, but hunger is the ticket that will take you there." When hiring a new person, you must look for hunger – hunger to learn more, hunger to develop and take the business to new heights, and hunger for the next step. A hungry person will always be looking for a way to grow.

Humility

It can be tempting to hire the industry rock star with all the credentials and the right contacts, but these people might not always be the best fit for your business. A humble person is more likely to listen to others, support those around them, be more emotionally intelligent, and work in harmony for the benefit of all.

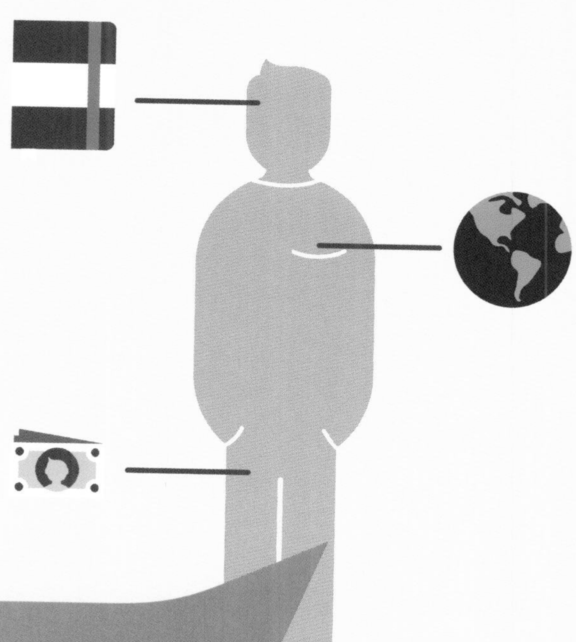

Chew on this:

How can you implement the three Hs of hiring in your business?

23. Entrepreneurship within a business: embracing intrapreneurship

What is an intrapreneur?

Richard Branson sums up intrapreneurship quite nicely. He says:

> "Many millions of people proudly claim the title 'entrepreneur.' On the other hand, a title that hasn't gotten nearly the amount of attention it deserves is entrepreneur's little brother, 'intrapreneur': an employee who is given freedom and financial support to create new products, services and systems, who does not have to follow the company's usual routines or protocols. While it's true that every company needs an entrepreneur to get it under way, healthy growth requires a smattering of intrapreneurs who drive new projects and explore new and unexpected directions for business development."

Why should you embrace intrapreneurship?

Intrapreneurship drives innovation

Encouraging your team to adopt the habit of sharing their creative ideas is simple to implement, but can lead to greatness. Get your whole team involved in things such as marketing your business – you may discover team members have been sitting on intrapreneurial innovations that could transform your business.

Retain your best assets

A Harvard study suggests 70% of successful entrepreneurs come up with their business idea while working for a previous employer, but don't share it as they feel like their boss isn't interested in their insights. Encouraging intrapreneurship will leave your team feeling inspired and valued, meaning they are much more likely to be fulfilled and stay in their role.

24. Influencing intrapreneurship in your business

'Intrapreneurs' are team members who actively look for ways to improve themselves and the businesses they work for. They ask questions, offer practical solutions, and encourage new ways of thinking.

Influencing a culture of intrapreneurship is particularly valuable because it encourages innovative thinking, improves business, and increases employee satisfaction through allowing them to contribute to the business. So, how can you influence intrapreneurship in your business?

Encourage collaboration
Many businesses suffer through a 'silo' culture, meaning teams work on their own without referring to others. Try putting different teams together to help come up with creative solutions to problems. This will help individuals to bounce around their ideas and work them into something useful.

Allow for feedback
Create an environment where continuous feedback is not just encouraged, but welcomed. This will help employees feel comfortable speaking out about their ideas.

Encourage healthy competition – This will help individuals to get creative and be ambitious.

Make risk-taking acceptable

Most businesses avoid risk at all costs for fear of failing, but just looking at the biggest entrepreneurs proves that risk is necessary for innovation. Develop a culture where small scale risk taking isn't shunned but encouraged, but also make sure that employees are well positioned to learn from their mistakes.

25. Taking the con out of conflict

Conflict is a good thing, and your business should embrace it. Now, hear me out.

Conflict is inevitable in business, as it is in life. Sometimes, individuals have very different viewpoints and this can't be avoided. The difference is how the conflict is managed.

When we talk about conflict, we might think of stormy silences, grudges, or even throwing punches. However, if your organisation encourages trust and openness, conflict doesn't always end up this way. In fact, it can be beneficial. If properly managed, we can take the con out of conflict and make it constructive.

You can manage conflicting thoughts and opinions through creating healthy environments where individuals feel safe to disagree. As a manager, acting as a mediator for these opinions, and letting others voice their feelings, can help your business generate new and exciting ideas which you might not have initially considered. This can help your business to push forward with innovative solutions when facing a particularly tricky task, rather than simply going with the 'done thing'. Building this kind of culture also encourages ownership and responsibility while discouraging blame and excuses through open dialogue.

Conflict is a good thing – learn how to manage it and you will likely find that you'll be involved in some very interesting discussions.

Chew on this:
Are you managing conflict in a way that encourages your team to be more open with their opinions?

26. The benefits of diversity

Could a lack of diversity in your business be holding you back? That's a possibility, according to a report into the effects of diversity in the workplace.

The Ruby McGregor-Smith review found that employment rates for people from BAME backgrounds were 12% lower than their white counterparts, and just 6% of employed people from BAME backgrounds reach top level management positions in their profession. However, the review also unearthed the fact that embracing a racially diverse workforce could have a significant impact on the UK economy. According to the report, increased diversity in business could see GDP increase by up to 1.3% a year, giving the UK economy a £24bn-a-year boost. And it's not the only report to suggest that diversity can benefit UK businesses in a positive way. An analysis of 2,400 companies by Credit Suisse showed that organisations with at least one female board member yielded a higher return on equity and net income growth.

So why can diversity help your business perform better?

A diverse team offers a broader range of culture and experience. This means that a diverse team can offer a wider range of perspectives, ideas, and approaches, some of which might be more successful than the 'done thing'. It also means that your team will better reflect your customer base, helping to build trust and empathy.

As Ruby McGregor-Smith put it; "The business case is there for all to see. But providing equal opportunities to people of all backgrounds is also, quite simply, the right thing to do."

Chew on this:
How could you embrace the benefits of diversity?

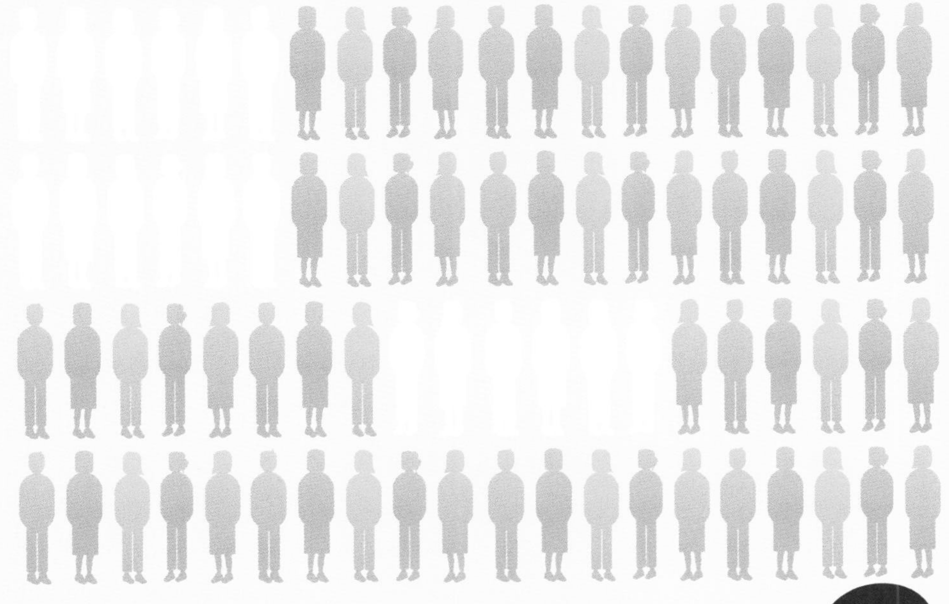

27. Unlocking the potential of a diverse team

Diversity can offer your business many benefits – from a wider range of ideas and skills, to a broader range of experiences, contacts, and knowledge to draw upon. With all these different ideas and energies present in a team, sometimes it can be difficult as a manager to know how to use them. Here are 4 tips for unlocking the potential of your team and harnessing the power of their diversity.

Unify under a shared purpose

People with different experiences and backgrounds are invariably likely to have different opinions on some things. While this is great for getting creative and encouraging innovation, it may sometimes cause tension or an inability to come to a solution. Ensuring that employees feel motivated by a shared common purpose while still being free to engage in debate means that they will be more likely to put differences aside and work together to achieve a goal.

Be welcoming and respectful

This can mean many things, from investing in diversity-related training for your team, to ensuring that you are always available for people to bring forward any concerns. Doing this will make sure that everyone in your team feels satisfied and welcomed. It is also important to respect different cultures and traditions, including the way that people dress and present themselves.

Encourage knowledge sharing

Knowledge sharing is key when it comes to harnessing the skills and knowledge of a diverse team. You might want to encourage a mentoring scheme that allows this, focusing on pairing together people with different backgrounds - for example young with old, or men with women.

28. Matching employee experience to employer brand

Have you ever hired somebody to fill a vacancy at your business, only to have them decide that the job just isn't for them? If your business is struggling with employee retention, it might be a sign that something is amiss. One thing that many organisations struggling with this problem fail to do is to ask themselves: **are we holding up our side of the bargain?**

When you're hiring for a job, it's important to advertise the things that make your business a great place to work. Perhaps you go out for lunch as a team on a Friday, or maybe you have a good programme in place to aid career development. Whatever it is, promoting these things is essential in attracting top quality candidates to the role.

But many businesses struggle to keep up with the promises they make - whether in a job advert, projected on social media, or claimed in company values. When a new recruit walks through the door on their first day, it's key that they get what they signed up for. If all the glitz and glamour falls away, and they are left with all the work and none of the rewards, what's to stop them from walking away? In today's world, it's even more important to ensure that you are providing a positive experience, as websites such as Glassdoor - which allows employees to leave reviews - can make it difficult to get the candidates through the door in the first place.

Keep your employees happy by ensuring that you do what you can to deliver on the promises you made at the beginning. Talk to them about your company values, and how they see themselves fitting in with their day-to-day role. Allow the people in your team to establish your employer brand, rather than having it dictated down from senior management. Encourage them to talk about what motivates and demotivates them while at work. Deliver on these areas consistently and ensure that expectation and promise match reality to develop an employer brand that is clear and honest, and you will attract the kind of people that will fit in well at your business, and will want to stay.

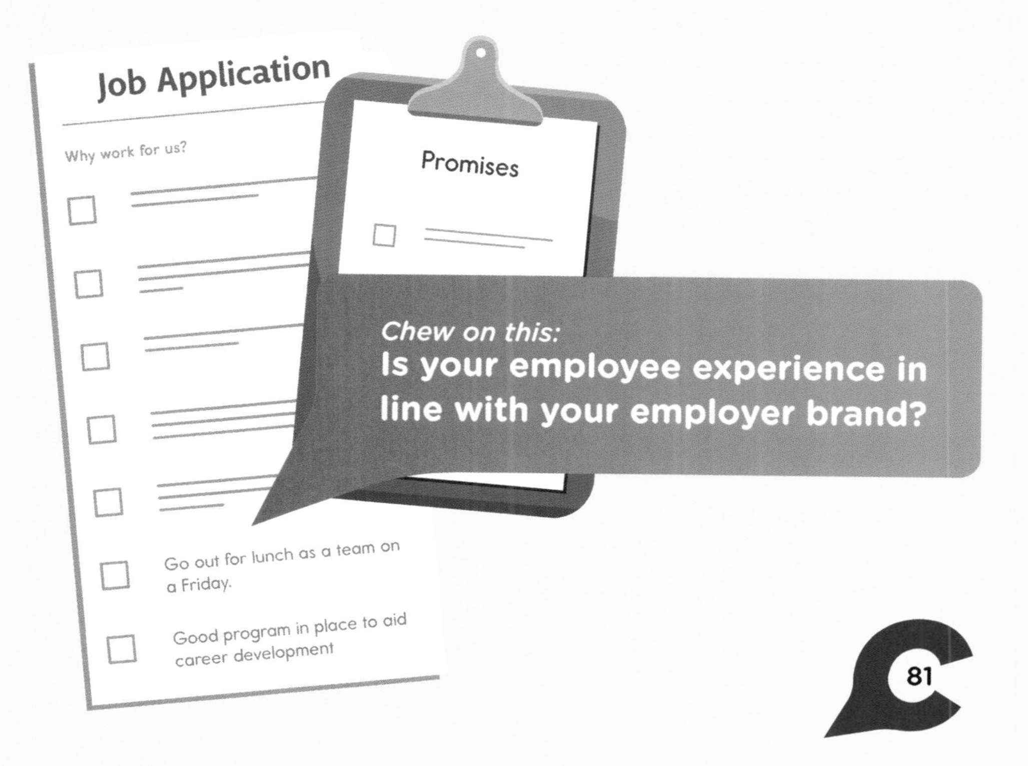

29. Setting the foundation for business transformation

What will your business look like in three years? What about five years? What changes will have been made? What innovations will you have championed?

Innovation and transformation are hot topics in business, and new technologies and methods of delivery are emerging at an impressive rate. True business transformation must go beyond simply reacting to current and emerging trends – you need to build a culture that has foundations to withstand ongoing change in the long-term.

So how can you do this?

Encourage dialogue
Create an ongoing discussion about innovation and transformation that spans across all areas of your business. Encourage employees to engage with new ideas and voice their opinions to create a culture of trust and willingness to embark on new ventures.

Create a long-term plan
Creating short-term goals with the right teams and reacting to change as and when needed is great, but you need to think beyond what's hot right

now. Work with your team to develop a vision for the future and a strategy for how you will get there. Encourage them to visualise what they want to be doing in the future and how they want to take part in transformation. This will create an environment where everyone is keen to work towards the next big thing.

Empower your team

A culture that promotes risk-taking, flexibility, and new ideas is likely to produce happy, empowered, and productive teams. Trust that your team will act in your business's best interests, and recognise them for their achievements when they do take a risk that pays off. This will encourage others to act in the same way.

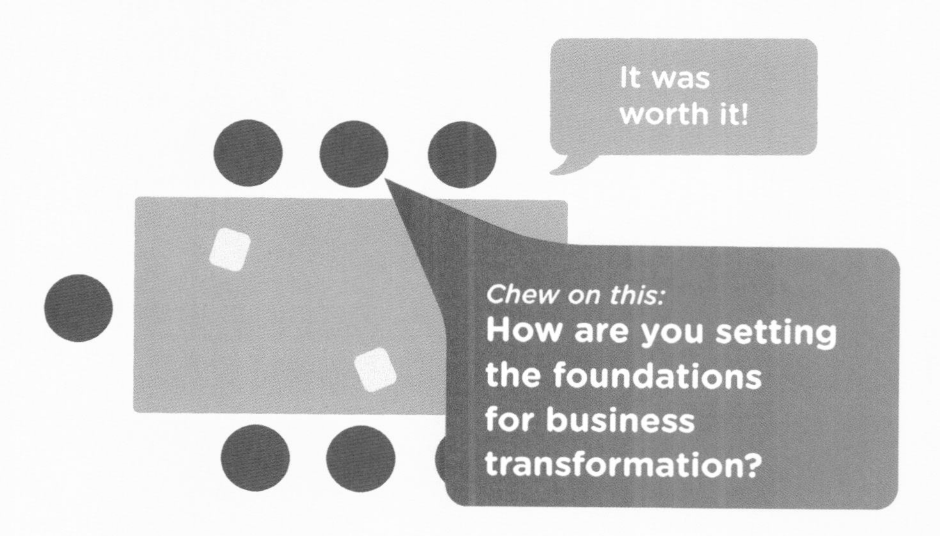

30. Netflix Culture: giving space to your team

What is 'Netflix Culture'? The idea comes from Netflix's policy which allows employees to take unauthorised time off and expense without approval. They believe that giving employees this freedom, trusting them to 'act in Netflix's best interest', will nurture innovation and creativity without bogging them down with mundane processes.

So why would a business want to adopt Netflix culture?

Typically, most companies curtail freedom and become more inflexible as they grow. This is because the larger an organisation is, the more it needs processes and rules to keep disorder at bay. These processes bring efficiencies, but they can curtail creativity and innovation as employees will need more approval to act on ideas.

Of course, some safeguards are good and necessary, such as those that might prevent a negative impact on the business, including processes relating to moral, ethical, legal, or financial practices. However, giving your employees the freedom to work flexibly and trusting them to act with self-discipline can encourage them to adapt quickly to shifts in the market – such as new technologies, what your competitors are doing, or emerging business models that could help the company grow. In allowing the freedom to work as they feel, and not restricting their creativity by requiring them to adhere to lots of unnecessary processes, you will find yourself with a team that can 'think outside the box', be flexible, and solve problems quickly and creatively.

Chew on this:

Could elements of Netflix Culture be adopted into your business?

31. Help! My high-performing team member has taken another job

If one of your best employees has thrown in the towel, it can be easy to blame a variety of possible causes. It's just that time of year where people need a change, or perhaps something better simply came along and it was all out of your power.

Or was it? Whenever an employee leaves your organisation, it's imperative to look inwards to find out whether there's anything that you could have done differently to stop it happening – especially if your relationship has been solid up until that point. Here are a few of the top mistakes businesses make which cause good employees to leave – and how to solve them.

Telling, not including

Business leaders are often emotionally charged and excited by every element of their work – their business is their baby, after all. But even the best and most committed employees aren't always 100% emotionally engaged, as they are likely to have other drivers outside of work. When rolling out new ideas, products, and values, it's crucial to involve your staff from the very beginning so that you have their buy-in from the outset.

Profit over purpose

What is your business here for? Communicating your purpose is key in employee retention, as a purpose creates an emotional connection between an employee and the work they're doing. This helps them to feel motivated and committed.

Cementing culture

Culture is important – but it's not set in stone. As your business grows, new people are likely to bring in fresh perspectives and new ways of working. And if a business can't evolve with its workforce, then it's likely to end up with a lot of dissatisfied people. Culture is more than just the words that you put on the wall – it's a living, growing organism. Measure your culture, check in on your employees' perspectives of it, and make sure that your business adapts its culture to the people that make it, rather than prescribing it to them.

The three pillars of sustainable business growth

Growth doesn't always look like growth. We can be at our most busy when our business growth is at its slowest, and sometimes we can hit a homerun and everything becomes exponential without us feeling like we're working hard at all. Whatever stage your business is at, things will probably get tough sooner or later. The world of business can be volatile, and because of this, many companies succumb to external factors such as changes in the market, or a sudden loss of clients. If you want to achieve sustainable growth, here are the three key things that you need.

32. Crunching the numbers: the first pillar of sustainable growth

33. Effective systems and processes: the second pillar of sustainable growth

34. A winning mindset: the third pillar of sustainable growth

35. Digging a little deeper: a winning mindset

36. Digging a little deeper: systems and processes

32. Crunching the numbers: the first pillar of sustainable growth

Growing a business requires a sustainable growth plan. There's a wealth of content from experts out there on this topic, but sometimes it can be a little overwhelming knowing where to begin. Sometimes, a simplified model can be useful in getting started, so I have outlined an overview of the three simple pillars that need to be in place to support sustainable growth. The first of these is numbers.

'If you can't measure something, then how can you improve it?'

Any objectives can, and should, be measured by numbers. This is because they can help you understand and improve many things, including:

Customers

Numbers can help you measure how many customers are loyal to your business, where your focus needs to be, and evaluate how effectively you translate leads into paying customers through processes such as web analytics.

Employee moral

How does your employees' behaviour contribute to your business's overall goals? They drive your business forward, so their morale is

key – a numerical value can help you see what things engage your employees and what things don't.

Efficiencies
Numbers can help you measure how much time is wasted due to things like technical breakdown and staff sickness to ensure you address any shortcomings and keep track of your results.

Financial performance
Of course! In order to assess your business growth, you'll need to be able to analyse factors such as your revenue per employee and return on investment, amongst others.

Internal processes
You need to ensure processes are allowing you to deliver projects on schedule and within budget, and the value generated by these projects. Numbers are the backbone and driving force of a business. In a world of constant change, being numbers-driven isn't an option, but a necessity.

Chew on this:
What things are you currently measuring regularly? What things could you measure to drive growth?

33. Effective systems and processes: the second pillar of sustainable growth

Systems and processes effectively ensure that your service is consistent, meets your desired standards of quality, and can be improved. Getting them right also means that your basic regulatory compliances are being met and your risks are managed. That's why having the right systems and processes are the second key pillar in achieving sustainable growth.

The right systems encourage innovation by promoting regular improvements whilst also ensuring maximised productivity and reduced wastage. They help your business to run as "lean and agile" as possible.

Systems and processes are a valuable tool in helping your customer service to be improved. For example, a 'Diary of Issues' is a system that drives quality and customer service, by allowing any issues to be followed up and reviewed, highlighting what can be improved in your customer service.

Without continuous improvement you are running on autopilot, with criticism providing the only reason for change. This is reaction as opposed to planning, which is simply not sustainable.

My suggested process is a consistent application of:

- **Appraise** - Reviewing the existing process
- **Amend** - Making the necessary changes
- **Approve** - Test the processes and confirm their usefulness with those involved
- **Apply** - Apply the newly approved process

In embedding a culture of improvement of your systems and processes, you will have a secure foundation on which you can grow and develop your business.

Chew on this:

How do you ensure consistency in your systems and processes?

34. A winning mindset: the third pillar of sustainable growth

This pillar is unlike the previous two in that it is less about the nuts and bolts and more about the importance of personal development and great leadership. A winnning mindset is important for sustainable growth because without it, you are likely to succumb to running on autopilot – or worse. But what does a winning mindset consist of? Surprisingly, it's less about being competitive and more about being willing.

Some tips for a winning mindset are:

- **Develop emotional intelligence** and self awareness
- **Seeking continuous growth** – and putting personal development first
- **Being really "open minded"** and taking ownership, accountability, and responsibility rather than being of being in a place of blame and denial. This will take you to a position of courage and peace

As the saying goes, the only constant is change. Business is constantly changing, and in addition, the way we learn changes. With this comes the acceptance that years of experience means less and less in this world. What was the case ten years ago might not exist anymore, and what is the case now, may not be the case three years from now.

If we are all open-minded, starting with getting rid of the 'I know' mentality, we will see that learning from others is as important as helping others learn. We can be both the mentor and the mentee.

A winning mindset gives you the ability to react and adapt quickly and to constantly evolve. Trying new things, understanding motivations, and taking action is key! A winning mindset would rather fail than not try at all - but most importantly, it understands the why.

35. Digging a little deeper: a winning mindset

Having emotional intelligence, being self-aware, seeking growth, taking ownership etc. can all be seen as 'softer skills' – things that are defined by how we think, and then the actions that follow. However, there are some concrete things that need to be defined before we can begin to develop a winning mindset. So how is a winning mindset developed?

Accurate self image

"Whether you think you can or whether you think you can't, you're right", goes the famous Henry Ford quote. There's plenty of research that suggests that no matter what external changes we make, our internal self image rarely changes. That's why it's important to understand ourselves at a deeper level. Be realistic, but also positive - what can and can't you do? What are your strengths and weaknesses?

Purpose

A business without a real purpose lacks a reason for being and therefore fails to motivate its staff. The same can be said about individuals - if we don't have purpose, where is our motivation going to come from? A purpose reflects positively on an individual, and in turn, that individual can inspire positivity in others – a whole business, even.

A purpose also ensures that the positivity we can feel from a winning mindset doesn't get wasted on positive thought, but becomes positive action. Having said that, the next thing to think about is...

Positive thinking

Business leaders are often subjected to a whole range of negative external influences, but it is often our role to be the person who leads and projects positivity to the wider team. This isn't just about saying the right things, but about making positive things happen within your business.

Passion

It is vital to remember and retain the passion that drove you when you first started your business. How passionate were you then? Did this not give you the drive to succeed?

A winning mindset is not made up of one thing, but many elements that come together to create greatness.

Chew on this:

What winning elements do you already possess? What do you need to develop?

36. Digging a little deeper: systems and processes

Systems and processes ensure consistency, efficiency, good customer service, quality, compliance and – crucially – continual improvement in your business. When it comes to sustaining business growth, these are all critical.

So what are systems and processes?

A process is essentially a working instruction in order to achieve a particular outcome. Think of a chef cooking – the recipe they use is their process; it tells them the ingredients they need, the order of mixing, the temperature to use, etc.

When these processes are used together consistently across your business, that's when they become a system.

Having an effective system is the easiest way to ensure that the work you produce is the best it can be, as having an orderly system allows you to achieve the following things:

- **Clarity** – A routine system of processes means your workflow is transparent and easy to follow
- **Cultivation** – Complacency is often a slippery road down to neglect. A clear set of processes allows you to analyse each step in its own right and develop the areas that need improvement.

- **Consistency** – As well as consistently great results, a routine way of doing things (and doing them well) means you'll achieve routinely good results. Simple really, but oh-so important.

The systems that you use depend on a multitude of factors, including your business, your goals, and what type of tasks you're doing on a daily basis. What's important, however, is that you have them in place.

Rethinking innovation

In order to help your business grow in terms of size and sales, it's important to ensure that you're growing in other ways. One of the most important factors in this growth is innovating and remaining relevant in your industry. However, innovation isn't simply jumping on the latest trends as soon as you can – it's also about transforming how your business works and making sure that you're always improving on what you're good at. This is not just about major changes, but making marginal gains which add up over time.

37. The myth of the first mover advantage

38. Why it's okay to copy your competitors

39. The merits of putting all your eggs in one basket

40. The importance of avoiding autopilot

41. Learn to learn

37. The myth of the first mover advantage

Let's begin with a story to illustrate the reason why being first in the race doesn't always give you the advantage. In the 1940s and 50s, Britain was regarded as a world leader in civil aviation. In particular, the first commercial jet airliner, the Comet, with its four engines making it capable of long haul flight, was regarded as the best of the best.

However, before too long, there were several catastrophic accidents in which the aircrafts appeared to fall out of the sky. Tests found that the unusual square shaped windows led to metal fatigue under the pressures of high altitude jet flight.

The Comet was later relaunched with round windows, but in that time, Boeing in the USA launched a rival, the 707, which would dominate the long haul civil airline market for the next decade and a half.

The 'first mover advantage' suggests that those who innovate and make the first move will be rewarded for their efforts. Naturally, we believe that a business that is first with a new product or service will do best as it is ahead of its competitors.

However, this is not always the case. In 2001, academics Peter Golder and Gerard Tellis found that companies often get limited rewards from being pioneers. Why? Being first comes with high risk, no benchmarks, and a market that might not be interested, whereas coming second gives you the opportunity to learn from the mistakes of those before you, to watch the market's reaction, and to allow the market to become more open to your ideas. Innovation and trying new things is key to growing your business - but so is learning from those who have gone before you and improving on what's been done before. When you're setting out a strategy for growing your business, be careful not to jump on the hottest new trend or product simply because it looks flashy. Think carefully about what steps you will take to get to where you want to be, what the risks and rewards are, and what you need to have in place should it not exactly go to plan.

What do you think of the first mover advantage? Is being the first to do something enough to guarantee your business growth in that area?

38. Why it's okay to copy your competitors

Here is one of the little-known secrets to business growth – you don't have to be different or the most innovative to win customers – just *better than your competitors*.

How can you do that? Let's just say a little inspiration goes a long way.

Ditch your USP: The chances are, your USP is not truly unique, as we have discussed previously. So stop trying to find what makes you unique and different from your competitors, and instead find what you're best at - even if it's something a competitor is good at too.

Research: Research what your competitors are doing, why they're doing it, and what they're achieving from it. Take note of what they're doing well that you could do better, but also capitalise on their weaknesses by making them your strengths.

Improve on competitors' concepts: Market the difference you can make to the consumer, rather than how you are different from your competitor. If you see a competitor doing something well, assess how you can improve on it to make a better service for your customers.

Know your strengths: Don't try to be another business. Remember the things that make your business great and don't neglect them. Doing something well will always beat trying to do something different.

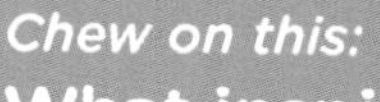

What inspiration have you taken from another business? How did it help you get to where you are now?

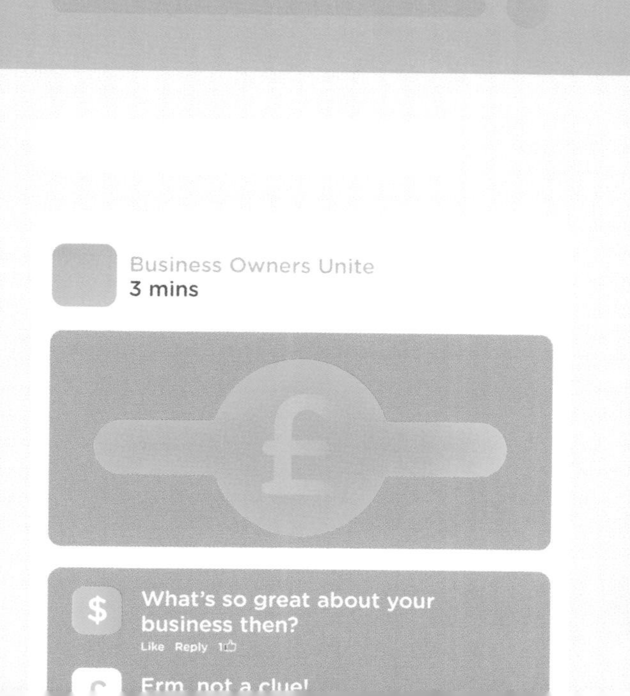

39. The merits of putting all your eggs in one basket

Proverbial wisdom tells us never to put all our eggs in one basket, but many business owners fall into the trap of looking to diversify when it is not something that will benefit them - particularly when their business is still growing and developing.

If you look at the big winners, you will realise that they specialise and stay focussed in one area.

Those businesses that fail are more often those which have scattered their capital. They have investments in this, or that, or the other, here, there and everywhere. In doing this, they have "scattered their brains" and find it difficult to keep focussed on making one thing - anything - work.

'Don't put all your eggs in one basket' is often wrong. For most of us, we should be saying **'put all your eggs in one basket, and then watch that basket.'** In doing so, you are much less likely to fail. It is easy to carry one basket, but he who carries three baskets instead of one will find he must put one on his head, which he will - of course - inevitably drop.

The great successes in life are made through focus. The man who is director in half a dozen banks, half a dozen railroads and four manufacturing companies is perhaps not as valuable or influential in his industry as the man who is simply director in fourteen banks.

There's always room at the top in every pursuit, and concentrating all your energy and thought is the only thing that will get you there.

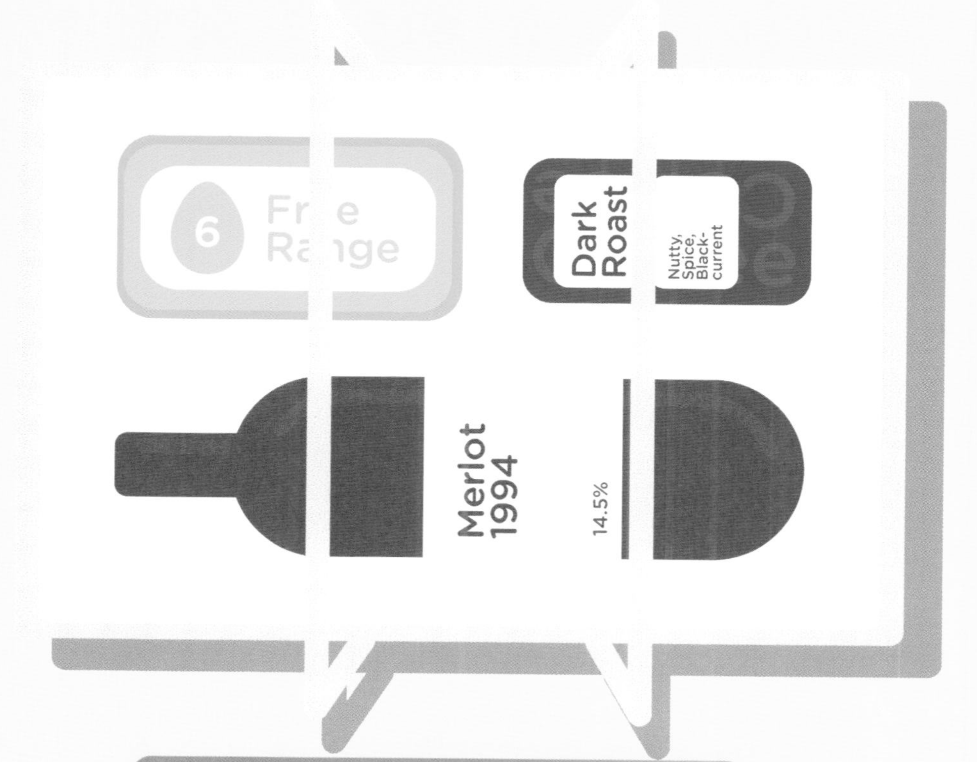

Chew on this:

Would you be better off to put all your eggs in one basket?

40. The importance of avoiding autopilot

It might be hard to conceive now, in the age of Apple, but there was a time when BlackBerry was the market leader in smartphone and mobile broadband innovation – in 2007, the company was valued at over $40 billion. However, less than a decade later in 2013, BlackBerry agreed to sell itself to Fairfax Financial Holdings Ltd for less than $5 billion. So what went wrong?

BlackBerry's issue, commenters agreed, was the business failed to innovate, allowing other smartphone companies – namely Apple – to rise up with new and exciting products and take BlackBerry's place as the market leader.

BlackBerry's decline is a great reminder of the importance of avoiding autopilot.

When you're in the lead, it's easy to forget to look at who's behind you. Businesses regularly fail because they start doing well and fall into the habit of being complacent. The only way to avoid this fate is to turn off autopilot and start actively thinking about what you can do to continue to get better.

For example, Blockbuster turned down an offer to buy Netflix in 2000 because CEO John Antioco thought Netflix was a "very small, niche business" – failing to see the potential of expanding from DVD rental to online streaming. And today, as you know, when we want to watch a movie on a Friday night, we no longer head to our local Blockbuster store, opting to log into Netflix instead.

Growing a business is all about innovation. When you spot a new trend, or your competitors start doing something different, analyse the reasons for it. Ask yourself what can you do that other businesses aren't doing yet or that you could do better? Even if you're a market leader, always think and behave like the number two, trying to catch up. This way, you will always be one step ahead and avoid getting stuck in a rut which sees your business plateau.

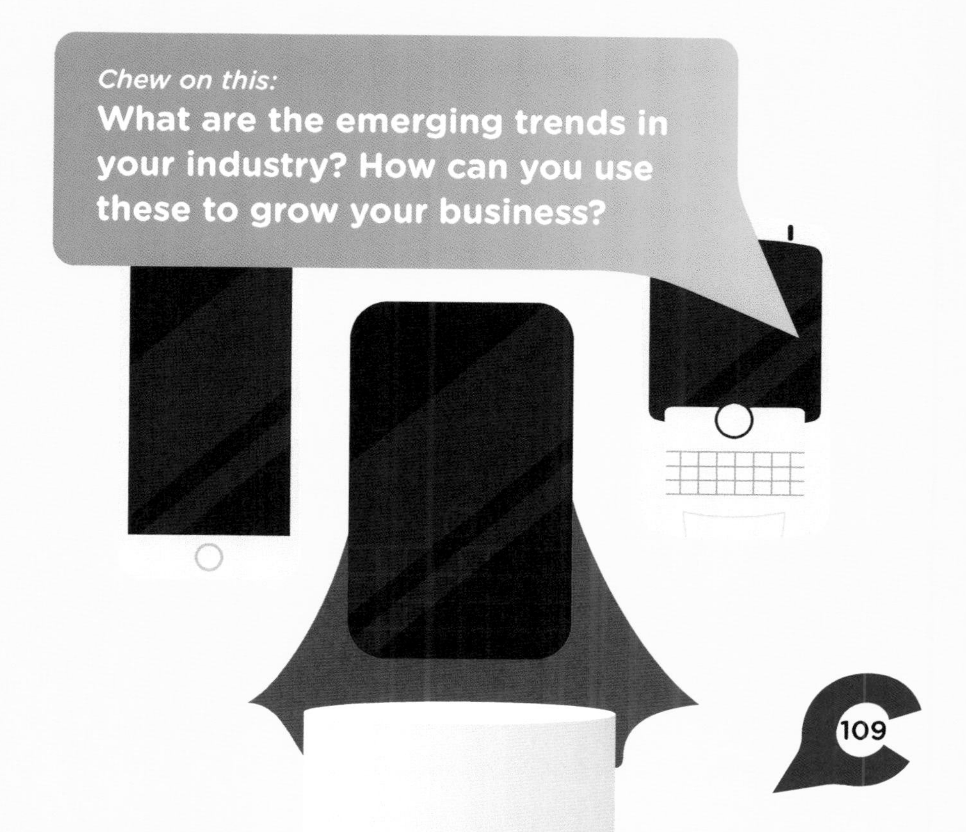

41. Learn to learn

Perhaps the most famous quote from author, futurist, and businessman Alvin Toffler is this: 'The illiterate of the 21st century will not be those who cannot read and write, but those who cannot learn, unlearn, and relearn'. But what does this mean?

Learning is perhaps the most important tool for any business person – from learning new skills to learning more about yourself, every new piece of information you absorb becomes part of the journey that led you to where you are today.

However, today's world – with its fast pace of social, cultural, and technological change – throws us one big curveball: everything – including what we have learnt – is constantly evolving. This means that what you may have learnt yesterday may not be relevant tomorrow. So what can we learn from this?

Today, experience and knowledge is less important than our ability to react and adapt to changing environments. In fact, having XX years of experience in a sector/industry plays an ever-decreasing role in measuring success. To combat this, we need to ensure that what we learn – the knowledge that we accumulate over time – and how we learn it, can all be used to help us to adapt to the challenges around us. If it does not, then what was the point in learning it?

The 70:20:10 learning model suggests that 70% of our learning should be from experience, 20% of our learning should be through others, and 10% should be learning through courses and structured programmes.

However, I feel that in order to be more effective, our learning should be distributed differently – **40% from experience, 40% from others (including mentoring and networking), and 20% from structured learning.** This balance means that we aren't relying on one method for the majority of our learning experience, rather looking for learning in more places. We need to place more emphasis than ever before on embracing different ways of learning – everything from webinars and reading, to peer learning and mentors – in order to stay relevant. Having a flexible approach to learning will help us to be flexible in other areas of our life too, which will help us to be more innovative. We need to not be so rigid in what we know and be open to new things and new ways of doing things. Why? Because the world is going to present these new ideas to us whether we embrace them or not. We must keep learning – but we must remember to unlearn and relearn at the same time. And that is perhaps the greatest learning of them all.

Chew on this:

How do you keep your knowledge fresh and up to date?

Selling your services

Even if you have a great service or product, selling it isn't always as easy as you might imagine. We live in a world with more information than ever, and so decision making is a much longer, and more complicated process than it might have been previously. To get people to become customers, you need a mix of good product or service, alongside strong relationships, effective marketing, and the right people.

42. Under-promise to over-deliver? Not a chance!

43. People vs. product: what is your customer buying?

44. The 7-11-4 rule

45. Digging a little deeper: the 7-hour rule

46. The 1% effect

47. Winning the review economy

42. Under-promise to over-deliver? Not a chance!

One of the keys to a successful business relationship is managing expectation. For some businesses, this means one thing – under-promising on results to over-deliver at a later date.

Of course, if you exceed expectations on key results your client is likely to be happy at the end of the project, right?

Under-promising to over-deliver is a terrible strategy for expectation management – and an even worse one for business development and client retention. In fact, by under-promising, you are potentially sabotaging your own chances at getting the work in the first place. But what about over-promising? It may seem tempting in the face of tough and unscrupulous competition, but promising the world before you've even started will land you in hot water – people will be only too willing to share a bad experience with others, potentially resulting in long term reputational damage.

So what should you tell that new client? The solution is clear – be as honest and as accurate as you can. It may cost you some work in the short term, but you will be rewarded in successful, long-term relationships, as well as having a client who is delighted with your ability to deliver exactly what they're expecting.

Promises

Chew on this:
Think of a time when you under-promised something to a client. How did that work out?

43. People vs. product: what is your customer buying?

Why do your customers buy from you?

Is it because of the quality product or services that you offer? Or is it because of the type of people you employ and the customer service that they provide?

You may be familiar with the process of customer journey mapping, which is the process of creating a visual representation of every experience your customers have with your business. This documents the story of a customer's experience from the moment they make that initial engagement to a hopefully long-term relationship.

Customer journey mapping can be very complex. Consider, for example, the fact that your customers are likely to come into contact with your business in a multitude of ways, including social media, advertising, customer service enquiries, or through using your products or services.

What's really at the heart of any purchase is the customer experience and how your business meets that need. That's why the people you hire are the key to turning an initial interaction into a life-long relationship. Your customers are human – so your business should be too. Providing an experience in which your customers feel that their needs are met and understood is likely to get you more die-hard fans than simply having a snazzy product or service.

44. The 7-11-4 rule

Marketers have identified three steps in the customer journey – starting with a stimulus, such as an advert, the 'first moment of truth', which involves the point of sale, and the 'second moment of truth', which involves the customer's experience.

A few years ago, Google added a new step into this model, called the 'zero moment of truth', which is where the customers educate themselves through research. The research by Google states that the buyer needs 7 hours of interaction with business or product, across 11 touch points, in 4 separate locations, before they make a decision to purchase.

This might sound like an insurmountable task, but the chances are if you don't have enough collateral in place, your customers are unlikely to engage with your business. Having a website is no longer enough, so how can you follow the 7-11-4 rule?

7 hours of contact could be face-to-face or it could be digital, such as using videos like demos and interviews, writing content such as white papers, blogs, guest posts, testimonials, or audio such as podcasts.

11 touch-points can be any of the resources where your customers can learn more about you, such as brochures, business cards, advertising, and your website.

Your 4 locations should be spread across a variety of places such as your website and social media, but also your office or shop, a networking event, or a third party website or review. The key to this is a strong focus on your content marketing strategy - are you repurposing content into different formats for different audiences? Are you ensuring that your SEO is up to scratch? Are you writing blogs for the right influential websites? Are you asking customers to leave a Google review? Ensuring that you do these simple things will help you follow the 7-11-4 rule and influence potential customers in the zero moment of truth stage.

Chew on this:
How are you performing against the 7-11-4 rule?

45. Digging a little deeper: the 7-hour rule

There's an unspoken rule amongst Japanese businessmen – you don't talk about doing business until after at least two rounds of golf.

The unspoken rule exists because during this time, each party can learn enough about the other to decide whether they might like to do business together – not necessarily from what they can offer in business terms, but whether they trust one another and enjoy working together.

Some experts suggest that any business or purchasing decision takes around 7 hours – about that of a couple of rounds of golf – before an individual makes a decision and therefore you should aim to get 7 hours of face time with them in order to build up a rapport before asking them to make a business decision.

However, in our busy lives, is it really feasible to be asking each of our business prospects out to lunch 7 times? Using that logic, the more successful you are at generating leads one month, the less successful you will be at generating leads the next month because you were too busy taking last month's leads out for coffee!

In this day and age, screen time is perhaps just as valuable as face-to-face time for many activities. For example, more customers will visit your website to find the answer to a question rather than popping into your office to ask. Therefore, the content you provide and the information you share with your business prospects is incredibly valuable. Consider how you share information with your prospects – linking them to a 15 minute video that you think they might find useful is in some ways far more effective than spending 15 minutes grabbing lunch with them when you are both too busy to discuss anything meaningful. Create and share content that makes a difference to your connections and you will soon see the hard work pay off.

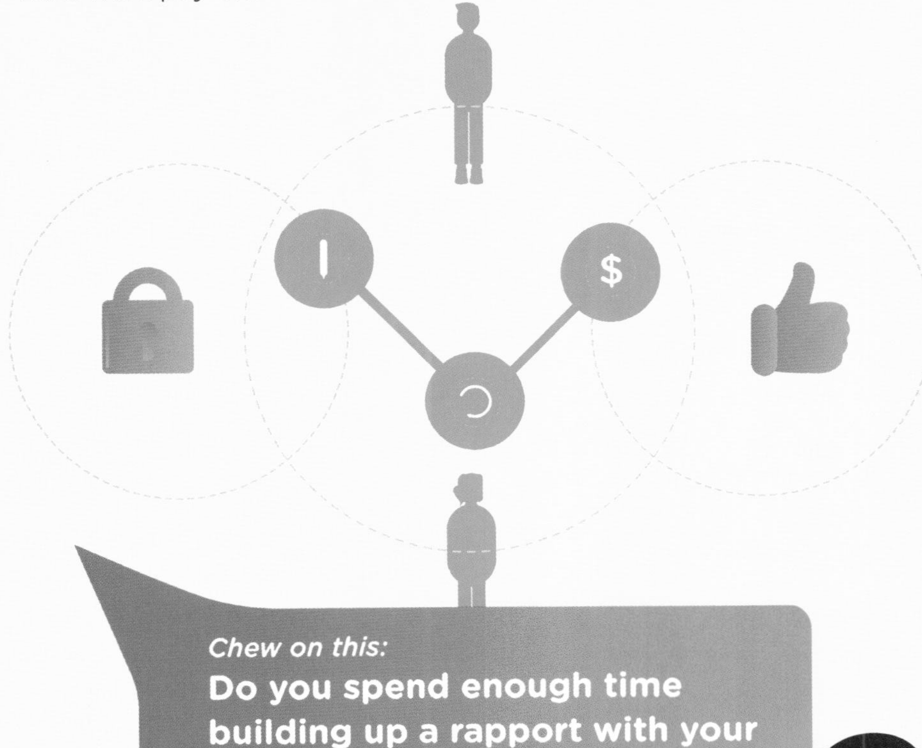

Chew on this:

Do you spend enough time building up a rapport with your prospective customers?

46. Greater Expectations

Customers' expectations are higher than ever – and often rightly so. In general, customers want more for less and increasingly better service. So how can we meet customer expectations without burning out?

We need to accept that we cannot alter the mind-set and expectations of our customers or make them care or expect less in any way. Instead, what we can do is understand what they do care about, what their main non-negotiables are, and how we can ensure our business delivers on our promise each and every time. We can do this by:

Understanding and defining our 'perfect' customer
We can't be everything to everyone – and nor should we aim to be. Instead, we need to know which customers are best matched to us. This comes down to having a deep understanding of who we are targeting, seeking to attract and retain their business, and aiming towards making them ambassadors of our business.

Understanding client expectations
We need to seek to understand all of our customers. If we get into their mind-set and not only try to understand them, but understand what they need from us in order to meet their expectations, we can then work on delivering on those expectations.

Experiencing the customer journey

We must also possess understanding of the customer journey within our business. Where did they find us? What were their initial interactions with us? What did those experiences feel like? What is the level of the service at the chalk-face?

Exceed to sustain

Beware of exceeding expectations in a way that isn't sustainable – you'll be taking one step forward and two back by doing so. Going the extra mile isn't about empowering one person – your aim should be for the customer to fall in love with the whole business and what you stand for rather than one person or division.

Consistency is king

A systemised business is a successful business. When you systemise your business, it runs itself. This creates consistency, and if clients experience consistently good service, we have a chance to retain and grow our relationship with them.

Chew on this:

How can you ensure that you consistently meet and sustain greater expectations?

47. The 1% effect

Price changes are often unavoidable. As your business grows, you'll likely be spending more on overheads, such as new staff or new technology. These things provide your customers with a better service, but it can still be hard to be confident when you need to tell your customers that you're increasing your prices.

So how can you do this?

It's all about understanding, identifying, and justifying the tangible and intangible benefits the customer may receive from a price increase. If, for example, you've added a new feature to a product, that's a tangible benefit and a customer would likely expect to see a price increase.

You should 'turn features into benefits'. Instead of simply saying, 'we can do this', turn it into 'we can do this which means you will get this'. This immediately makes it about the customer and helps them see what they will receive as a return on their investment.

There is an undeniable benefit that a simple 1% price increase can make to your business. It may not seem like much, but increasing your prices by 1% can have a minimal impact on your customers, but maximum impact on your business.

For example, would you stop reading your favourite magazine if the price went up by approximately 1% from £3.80 to £3.84? Probably not. So why would your customers not pay an extra 1% for an improved service or product?

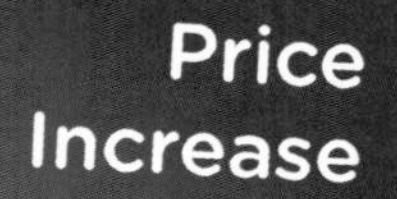

Run away

Chew on this:
**Do you think you are pricing your services correctly?
Is it time for a change?**

48. Winning the review economy

The world runs on reviews.

Think about it – when you want to get a taxi to the train station, you'll probably get an Uber where you'll review your driver.

If you want to go on holiday, you'll read reviews of hotels before you book, or you might even stay in an AirBnB where you'll be reviewed as a guest.

If you want to go out to eat, you'll probably check local restaurant reviews on TripAdvisor first. And if you're looking for a new job, chances are you'll tidy up your LinkedIn profile and ask a trusted colleague to leave you a recommendation.

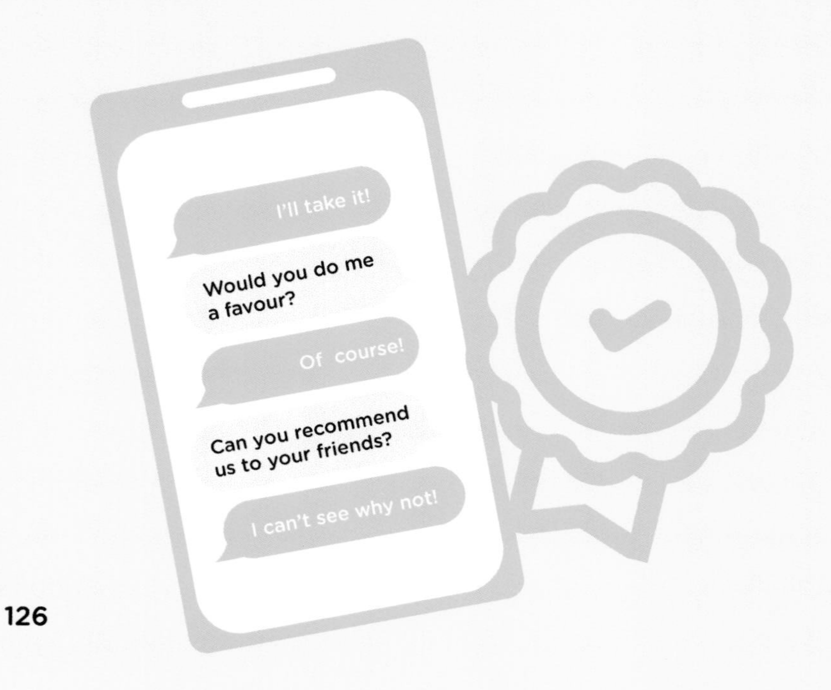

As we showed with the 7-11-4 rule, most consumers spend lots of time researching a product or service before making a purchase. So how can you ensure that your business ends up with glowing reviews that entice other customers and contribute to your business's growth?

In the review economy, you have to have a plan. There's no time for hoping somebody leaves a positive review on Google My Business. Every interaction you have with your customer is a chance to make an impression, but to win the review economy you must remember that you're only halfway done when you sell your product. You must measure the value you give your client and ensure that it is enough to make them recommend you to others. How do you do this? You simply ask.

Once you've sold your product or service, ask your customer if they are happy with it and whether they'd recommend it to a friend. If they are, ask them to do just that – you'll be surprised how difficult it is for them to say no once they realise they have no reason not to.

Chew on this:

How do you ensure positive reviews about your business? How do you deal with any negative reviews?

The attitude for achievement

We started this book by looking at you, and we'll finish it by looking at you. Why? Because as a business leader, you're the driving force behind your organisation's success. The right attitude can go a long way when it comes to making positive change or reaching goals, and it's even more important to have when things go wrong. If you take one thing away from my book, I hope it's a different mindset – one geared towards achievement.

49. Never take no for an answer

50. It's not about work/life balance, it's about work/life choice

51. The power of caring

52. Be better, be recognised, be an award-winner

49. Never take no for an answer

It is wise advice to never take no for an answer in business. But why?

When someone says 'no', it may not mean that the answer is no. In fact, what it could mean, is that you have not done enough work to get the answer 'yes'. Here are a few things to consider that can help you to never take 'no' for an answer.

If someone says 'no', you have to educate them
Often people say no when they do not understand – they are too busy to hear what you are saying, they are not knowledgeable enough to say yes, or you haven't explained yourself well enough. Take this opportunity to reframe your proposal, to educate them on the benefits, or to ask a question that will give you a response that they won't be able to dispute.

If someone says 'no', you're asking the wrong person
Sometimes people say no because they are not the right person to say yes. They might not have the authority or the budget to take your offer on. Targeting this person can waste lots of time and resource. Instead, take time to do your homework and make sure that when you ask the question, you're asking the person that can say yes.

If someone says 'no', you're not thinking about their needs
When pitching something, you're really proposing a solution to two problems rather than one – the solution to what you need, and the solution to what they need. When someone says no, it's likely you've been thinking more about the former than the latter. Spend time thinking about where the overlap is – what do you have in common? What things do you both care about? But most importantly, listen. Ask questions. Understand. Then, using your new found knowledge, ask again. This time, they're likely to say yes.

50. It's not about work/life balance, it's about work/life choice

We often talk about work/life balance, but what if we told you that there was no such thing?

Jack Welch, former General Electric CEO, has been quoted as saying: 'There's no such thing as work-life balance... There are work-life choices, and you make them, and they have consequences.'

Author Stephen Covey raises a similar point in his book 'The 7 Habits of Highly Effective People'. He tells the story of a student who asked if he could miss one of his classes because he had to to go to a tennis lesson. When asked why he had to, he replied "Why, they'll kick me off the team" – a consequence he said that he would not like to endure.

Covey replied, "In other words, you choose to go because you want the consequence of staying on the team. What will happen if you miss my class?" The student replied that he would miss the learning. "That's right", Covey said. "So you have to weigh that consequence against the other consequence and make a choice. I know if it were me, I'd choose to go on the tennis trip. But never say you have to do anything."

"I choose to go on the tennis trip," the student meekly replied.

"And miss my class!?" Covey replied in mock disbelief.

The phrase work/life **balance** suggests equal weight given to both parts, but people take different approaches to their work depending on a variety of factors such as where they are in their career path, their health or age, family situations, financial reasons, etc. Work/life **choice** empowers an individual to focus on what is important to them at any given moment. In business, our priorities shift all the time, and we are often faced with choices. Every choice has a consequence – that's just the nature of life. The key to success is to recognise this, prioritise, and adjust accordingly.

51. The power of caring

Successful business big-shots are stereotypically shown as hard, shrewd individuals who are willing to do anything to succeed. This attitude, however, is perhaps further from the truth than you might think. It might not be an obvious tool to equip yourself with in the business world, but the ability to care and show emotion is perhaps one of the most powerful things you can do to help you be successful.

Why?

The reasons can be summed up in the following expression:

'They don't care how much you know until they know how much you care.'

In life, individuals are drawn to those who they can genuinely connect with, and the act of doing business is no different. If you can show that you truly care about your customers, they will be more likely to value your business and use it again.

A truly special business goes beyond simply providing a good product or service by demonstrating in word and deed that it really cares. Next time you are interacting with a potential customer, think about what problems you are solving for them, show that you are truly passionate about helping fix those problems, and explain that's why you do the work that you do.

Chew on this:

How have you shown that you care recently?

52. Be better, be recognised, be an award-winner

No matter what business you are in, an award is a transformative opportunity. However, many of us are reluctant to enter our business for awards not only because the process can be time-consuming, but also because we fear putting in the time and effort only to not come out on top. However, there are plenty of reasons to enter your business for an award – not least because you might win it. All that you need is to understand how the process can help you to achieve and the confidence to put yourself forward.

You'll stand out

Winning an award, or even being nominated, enhances your reputation and sets you apart from your competitors. It also reminds your current customers that they made a great choice by working with you and lets you say with confidence that you are one of the best in the business.

It'll boost your team

An award win or nomination will not only help you attract the best talent, but will help your existing team to feel inspired and motivated, helping them to adopt an attitude for achievement and to be more tenacious.

You can reflect on your business

Putting your business forward for an award gives you the opportunity to be introspective and reflect on the nature of your business – what it does well, what it's improving on, and what you should be celebrating.

It will grow your confidence

When it comes to awards, you have to be in it to win it. Don't be led by fear of competitors, even if they are more established and better known than you. It can be intimidating but even getting to the position of being nominated alongside them can improve your status and help encourage you to further adopt a winning mindset.

Chew on this:
How would winning an award inspire you and your team to keep winning?

About the author

Safaraz Ali began his career in the financial services sector and since 1999, has been involved in business of one type or another. He is the Head of Pathway Group, an organisation committed to changing lives through skills and work.

Safaraz created Pathway2Grow, whose tagline is 'Network, Learn and Grow', with a vision to conduct business networking differently. Pathway2Grow is a vibrant network with ambitions to serve business communities nationally by running free events in partnership with business owners who wish to grow their business by raising their personal and business profile in a proven method.

Through the vehicle TCI Pathway Ltd, Safaraz offers independent strategic advice and investment for private businesses specialising in social care, education and the training sectors. It offers support and guidance in developing growth strategies, executing them, raising funds and management.

He has been a judge for the prestigious Great British Entrepreneur Awards, the Birmingham Awards, the UK Government's National Apprenticeship Awards and is the Founder of ThinkFest Events, the people behind the Asian Apprenticeship Awards, the Business Book Awards, and the Adoption and Foster Care Awards. Safaraz is also the author of 'Canny Bites: 52 Bites of Business Wisdom for Leaders and Entrepreneurs', the first in the Canny Bites series.

You can contact Safaraz on his social media feeds:
www.linkedin.com/in/safaraz
www.twitter.com/SafarazAli
www.youtube.com/user/safaraz

Praise for Canny Bites: What people are saying...

"This little masterpiece surpasses the competition in so many ways. It's genuine, relevant, adaptable and fun."

"In a world of information overload, pressure to perform and unreasonable expectations, 'Canny Bites' is a brilliant piece of writing ... Each treatment is devoid of fluff and fill; resulting in practical, usable tips and strategies for improved performance."

"Safaraz has a remarkable method of delivering key messages in an artful and memorable way. A must-have for any business owner or leader who wants to make a difference."

"Canny Bites is full of practical, useful and interesting questions, idea,s and thoughts that will guide any business leader trying to be better."

"Presented in an easily digestible format that allows you to dip in and out when you need to challenge your views and perspectives."

"Canny Bites is full of bursts of practical and memorable knowledge that can be easily applied in your world of work."

"A book that engages you from beginning to end. A book that is bold, direct and real."

CannyBites

Another 52 bites of business wisdom for leaders and entrepreneurs

The second book in the 'Canny Bites' series, *'Canny Bites: Another 52 bites of business wisdom for leaders and entrepreneurs'* is packed with practical business tips for today's professionals. Covering everything from working with a business consultant to inspiring intrapreneurship in your business, and answering difficult questions such as 'what is a team for?' and 'are you cut out to run a business?', Safaraz Ali's follow up to *'Canny Bites: 52 bites of business wisdom for leaders and entrepreneurs'* dives into the details and know-how needed to be a successful business professional.

What readers are saying about 'Canny Bites':

"An excellent read for any business owner or entrepreneur looking for more success in their professional life. Well presented into easily accessible "bites" so it can be read on the go or whenever you've got a few minutes free for some self-development!"

- Bradley Edwards

"Safaraz has obviously thought long and hard on how to set out these Canny Bites so that they can be used by anyone, from novice business men to old timers to entrepreneurs of all ages, and it is a welcome addition to my library"

- Peter Stone

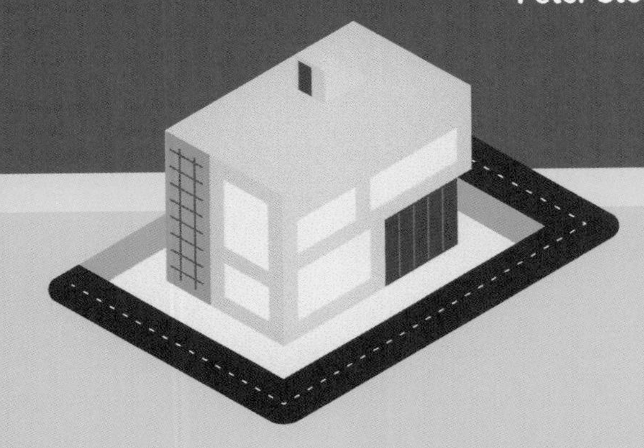

22092504R00080

Printed in Great Britain
by Amazon